"It took me 14 years to reach the executive level at Weyerhaeuser. If I would have had what I call "Jack's How-To Book", I could have reached my goal 3 to 5 years sooner. That's a big difference!

"Jack's book, which I read pre-publication, should be in every manager's library and should be assigned reading in all business schools."

—*Darrel Stutesman, Director of HTI Polymer, Inc.;*
formerly, Sales Executive at The Weyerhaeuser Company

"I had the privilege of having Jack as a manager and mentor during my years at Microsoft. He was responsible at the time for the IT Pro audience marketing team. When I think about Jack, I see first a great team leader who cared deeply about his team and beyond, who took the time to listen to and learn about his people, and understood how to inspire them.

"Jack's approach to work was both very strategic, yet practical, and his inclusive management style made for an amazing working environment where everyone's contributions were listened to and valued."

—*Angela Paraboni Viesse, Principal Consultant*

"I'm not surprised that this book's concept is unique. I love it, and I wish that I'd had it in my hands early in my management career – but I was luckier because I had Jack as my manager and personal coach."

—*Rob Epp, CEO/founder of TopGlides.net; formerly,*
Director of online properties at a Fortune 500 company

"Jack Litewka is the consummate C-Suite consultant to C-Suite professionals-in-the-making. The depth of his experience continues to spur innovation with proven techniques that benefit my division heads to run profitable business units. It's about time that Jack share with the enlightened masses his particular skillset. He articulates for the next CEO generation how to run a company transparently. A *must* read…"

—*Alex Anderson, Managing Partner, AG Venture Partner*

"In my more than two-decade career, Jack is the best manager that I have ever had. He is genuinely interested in, supportive of, and encouraging to his employees, and is incredibly smart about business and communication. But the reason he is a *fantastic* manager is that he constantly assesses the skills and abilities of his employees, praises them for their efforts and achievements, and then pushes them to progress even more.

"I learned and grew more in my time with him than with any other manager or mentor."

—*Alison Ellard, Sr. Creative Professional; formerly, Art Director and Sr. Product Manager at a Fortune 500 company*

"I had the honor to work with Jack when I was leading a strategy consulting team in Microsoft's Worldwide Services division. Jack is one of the best and most effective people managers/leaders I've met – due to his incredible intellectual power, business acumen, and impeccable ethics. Jack is strategic: he genuinely cares about the bottom-line business results and the people involved in change management. He understands them, empowers them, and makes sure his team is successful."

—*Beny Rubinstein, Digital Transformation Solution Sales Lead at a Fortune 500 company; formerly, President & CEO, Acelera Partners*

"As a Direct Report of Jack at Microsoft, I can say he was the best manager I had (and I had a lot of them). Attributes that made Jack a pleasure to work for were his honesty, integrity, listening skills, team-building skills, coaching skills, and ability to develop a clear vision, mission, and supporting goals for and with his teams."

—*Scott Smernis, Dealer Principal, Sound Harley-Davidson; formerly Director of Program Management at Microsoft Corporation*

"Having Jack as my first manager when I relocated from Argentina to the United States was fundamental for the successful career I now have. Jack is an extremely well-rounded manager who has mastered how to put people at the center of success. He defined a clear vision and strategy, and implemented a plan to get there."

—*Gustavo Basualdo, Sr. Program Manager at a Fortune 500 company*

"Jack was a calming voice in a shit-storm of insanity."

—*Stephanie Weeks, Program Manager, Technical Writer*

"Jack's wise, insightful and RELEVANT counsel – honed through his experience being an entrepreneur, advisor to start-ups, and being a senior manager in a global tech mega-firm – brought us through the difficult days that every business, entrepreneur, and start-up encounters. His patience, encouragement and desire to see us succeed were evident in his diplomatic and direct communication style. He was a GODSEND to us!"

—*Makedah Shartukar, Co-Founder & CEO, BiLD Corporation, and Vivian Stone, Co-Founder & COO, BiLD Corporation*

"This book is a masterpiece. I enjoyed reading every page of it. The insight and wisdom it contains are invaluable, and although I'm a very experienced manager, I learned a lot from reading it – and had more than a few *'Duh! I wish I had known/done that'* moments.

"This book is filled with a unique combination of highly practical advice that can be applied on a day-to-day basis and sage wisdom on the existential experience of being a manager that reflects a life lived carefully, deliberately, and with the kind of candid self-reflection to which most of us can only aspire."

—*David Wertheimer, Deputy Director for Strategy, Planning & Management, Global Foundation*

"Jack has been one of the most amazing managers of all times. Our projects over the 3 years that we worked together had numerous 1.0 versions with plenty of ambiguity, chaos, and lack of clarity and direction. Jack understood how to funnel the team through the noise to get us clarity and heading in a successful direction. When I had the bright idea to patent one of the features our team had developed, Jack figured out how to maneuver through the numerous attorneys and mounds of paperwork to get us two patents."

—Bella Acharya, Global Business Development at a Fortune 500 company

"Jack's mentorship played an important part of my pre-execution routine, when I needed help understanding the possible consequences of a decision, before I started acting on it. The depth of his management experience allowed him to look at a situation with a rounder and more critical perspective than mine."

—Jacob Motola, Senior Project Manager, Sales Operations

"I had the pleasure of working both with and for Jack in the early 2000's at Microsoft. It was a very challenging time in the company's history, with turmoil from outside the company matched by turmoil within. Mid-level management was often caught in the cross-fire, and Jack did an outstanding job keeping team cohesion and morale.

"One of Jack's great qualities was transparency: no matter how bad things got, he didn't sugar-coat matters and kept everyone focused on the important issues. As one of Jack's direct reports, I learned a number of tools and techniques that I carry with me still."

—Steve Murchie, CxO, Envision Technology Partners

"Jack was my manager for 4 years. Later, when I decided to move into management, Jack was the first person I turned to as a mentor. I've learned so much from him, especially the importance of making sure the people on my team know how much their contributions are appreciated.

"I learned from Jack that creating a culture that values honesty, inclusion, and collaboration puts a team in a great situation. From the small acknowledgements to the most careful strategic decisions, Jack taught me to understand the importance of being a thoughtful manager."

—*Paulette McKay, Sr. Content Publishing Manager at a Fortune 500 company*

"Jack has honed his management skills to the level of mastery, both by looking back and learning from his many experiences and by looking at the present-day challenges and opportunities to determine how to make managers successful. His approach is to share his perspective with you in a thoughtful and easy manner, with your best interests at the core.

"Jack's book provides the insights to accelerate the learning and minimize the pain that we all go through as part of the journey to become good managers."

—*Peter Rakoczy, President, Trillium Point Business Solutions*

"As a brand new second-line manager, I struggled with the right level of delegation, oversight, and direct touch that I should have with skip-level reports. Jack was a great mentor during this time and helped me achieve a balance between oversight and meddling."

—*Ines Vargas, Director, Global Partner Services at a Fortune 500 company*

"Jack has a unique management style that brings out people's best. It is an amazing ability to inspire and motivate his teams to deliver exceptional results. He builds on each individual's strengths, and fosters an environment where people collaborate to overcome business challenges. I really appreciated how he gave his teams the right level of guidance and a great deal of autonomy to own their work."

—Sassan Saedi, Vice President, Fortune 500 company; formerly, Head, Channels and Partnerships for a start-up

"Jack is truly interested in people's backgrounds, perspectives and opinions. Through this inquisitiveness and resulting wealth of knowledge he is capable of taking a diverse set of individuals and shaping them into a highly collaborative team able to take on the most complex problems and deliver high-quality solutions that transform organizations. Above all Jack is a mentor able to bring out the best in people, and foster a culture of trust and friendship."

—Remco Stroeken, Sr. Marketing Manager at a Fortune 500 company

"Jack's leadership style was a powerful demonstration that you can be an effective manager while still being true to yourself. That was a great managerial lesson for me. He didn't speak in platitudes or talk at you – he listened. He fostered a true spirit of two-way collaboration. He was highly attuned to the individuals that made up his team and was able to tailor his approach to guide a diverse set of personalities while at the same time bringing them together as a cohesive unit."

—Don Hall, Marketing Consultant; formerly, Director of Marketing at Microsoft

"Jack taught me that quality work does not have to be perfect work. Shipping something good is better than not shipping at all. This wisdom is daily reflected upon as I lead my teams through tough situations and tight timelines."

—Eric Sabetti, Director, UX and Product Management at a Fortune 500 company

"Jack Litewka is the Gold Standard for managers in my professional career. His intentional and thoughtful approach to the design and engineering of his teams has been a continual source of inspiration ever since I reported to him."

—David Kaill, Business & Technology Consultant

"During the 4 years that Jack and I were peers, we met regularly to discuss the corporate culture around us and how we could influence it as well as how to lead our respective teams more effectively. I found Jack to be deeply and intuitively anchored in understanding that culture is the sum of employee and manager behaviors that are understood by everyone to be normative.

"Any advice that Jack gives is valuable and will have strong positive impact. I strongly recommend this book to anyone who cares to lead their team effectively while skipping over most mistakes that new (and experienced) managers tend to make if left to their own devices. (Note: I've already noted a few practices from his semi-complete draft to incorporate in my behaviors... and I've had a number of managerial roles over the past 20 years.)"

—Thierry Paquay, Sr. Director at a Fortune 500 company

THE
SOPHISTICATED
MANAGER

The Sophisticated Manager: A Guide to Success

ISBN 978-0-9982964-0-1

eISBN 978-0-9982964-1-8

Printed in the United States of America

Cover Design and Illustration: Hannah Adams, hannah@cadmiumyellow.com

Interior Design and Layout: Stories to Tell Books, www.storiestotellbooks.com

Published by Out-of-the-Box Press

Berkeley, CA

http://sophisticated-manager-jack-litewka.net

Feedback, queries, and requests can be sent to the author: jack@jacklitewka.com

Contents

PREFACE

In mentoring dozens of managers over the years, I've learned a lot about what *undercut their confidence*, what they *felt unprepared to do*, what issues *caused them the most angst*, what they saw as *their biggest roadblocks*, in what areas they had *significant gaps in experience and knowledge*, and what were the *common mistakes they made*.

Certain themes came up again and again as I listened to their painful tales of the crises they were facing – and those themes, those pain points, are the heart and soul of this book and what I focus on. The recurring thought I had was that if managers learned how to do some things that they now have difficulty with in a world-class manner, they would be able to avoid much pain, anxiety, and serious missteps – and that thought inspired me to write this book.

Here are some of the topics that you will read about in this book:

- You will learn *some of the positive things that are *must-do's** if you are a recently-hired manager.
- You will learn *how to identify potential pitfalls* and *how to avoid them.*
- You will learn *how to think about the depth and breadth of your role.*
- You will gain *a deeper understanding of what you need to do to create a high-performance team.*

And, of course, much much more...

Mentoring has been among the most rewarding activities that I have had in a career spanning 40+ years – and this book is a form of one-to-many mentoring. It provides not only the *"what"* to do and the *"how"* to do it, but also the *"why to do it this way"*. That deeper understanding of the *"why"* is one factor that sets this book apart from other management books.

I want to continue the tradition, begun long before me, of nurturing the next generation of Great Managers. ***The Sophisticated Manager: A Guide to Success*** is my offering to that tradition – a tradition that I hope *you* will honor when you feel ready to do that – by mentoring those who will want to benefit from your experience.

IN THE TRENCHES...

(*aka* Lessons from the Real World)

This is an "in the trenches" book, focusing on real issues that managers – first-time managers as well as experienced managers – grapple with when they take on a managerial position. This book tells you *how* to do certain things that managers struggle with (rather than just telling you, in general terms, *what* you're supposed to do). I draw on my own experience and also on the experience of having both mentored and learned from many managers over the years, which made clear the ways in which managers get themselves into trouble.

This book contains real-life experiential "data" – hard-won knowledge about which soft-skill techniques and strategies are effective in the workplace.

This book does not try to cover everything that a manager needs to know. It does not list all the "should do's" – lists upon lists of all the myriad activities that a manager must handle. Instead, it zeroes in on how best to accomplish certain difficult tasks in a world-class manner. It provides guidance on the best way to address dicey situations and how to avoid serious mistakes that I've seen managers make, again and again, that undermined their credibility – missteps that often took many months to recover from (and full recovery sometimes did not happen).

My hope is that the down-and-dirty discussions and how-to guidance in this book will increase your ability to *deftly handle difficult situations* and, perhaps more importantly, will also help you to *avoid getting into trouble* in the first place.

You have in your hands *The Sophisticated Manager: A Guide to Success*. Use it wisely – and you will reach your goals while avoiding unnecessary suffering.

How to Read This Book

You can read this book in a variety of ways, depending on your role and your situation. For example:

New managers should read the next section *(below)* – *"Tips for New Managers Reading this Book"*.

Somewhat experienced managers who have been in a managerial role for at least, say, 6 months, should look for chapters that are most relevant or urgent right now.

Very experienced managers can hunt for unique techniques and tips that are not already part of their bag of tricks.

Tips for New Managers Reading this Book

For the New Manager – meaning those who have recently stepped into or are about to step into a manager's role – there are *must do* activities that should occur during the first 4 weeks on the job. These tasks can be found in Appendices 1-4, containing the "Mandatory Activities" for Weeks 1-4. Those Appendices focus on certain activities that New Managers often don't think of or often overlook or mistakenly believe that they are back-burner Priority 2 activities, when they need to Priority 1 activities.

Chapters that will be especially useful to New Managers and should be considered as *required reading* are:

- *Chapter 3:* "What Type of Soft-Skill Mistakes Is a New Manager Likely to Make"
- *Chapter 4:* "What Is the Key Responsibility of a Manager?"
- *Chapter 5:* "Creating Conditions that Allow Your Direct Reports to Succeed"
- *Chapter 6:* "The Day *Before* You Start a Job as a Manager"
- *Chapter 7:* "Weekly 'Mandatory' Activities"
- *Chapter 8:* "Your First Team 'Gathering'"
- *Chapter 10:* "How to Run Effective Team Meetings'"
- *Chapter 11:* "Your *First* 1-to-1 Meeting with *Your* Manager"
- *Chapter 12:* "Your *First* 1-to-1 Meeting with Each of Your Direct Reports"
- *Chapter 13:* "The Art of *Recurring* 1-to-1 Meetings with Your Direct Reports"
- *Chapters 18-39:* "Hiring Great People" (read *only if* you have open headcount that you need to fill; if you don't have open positions, you can read these chapters when it becomes timely)
- *Chapter 53:* "Developing a Communications Strategy"
- *Chapter 62:* "Email No-No's"
- *Appendices* 1-4 – "Mandatory Activities" for Weeks 1-4

Depending on your situation and experience, other chapters might also be "required reading". You'll figure it out.

The Order of Chapters in this Book

The topics in this book could have been arranged in a variety of ways, each good in its own way. I chose to begin with those issues that a manager is most apt to deal with almost immediately. For example, meetings start happening right away, whereas hiring might be immediate or might be many months or years in the future (depending on whether there is budget for new positions or whether a Direct Report leaves your team, thereby creating an open headcount).

Recommendation: Study the Table of Contents. You can then decide whether you want to read this book from front to back or whether you'd prefer to jump around and focus on those chapters that are most relevant to you right now.

PART ONE

THE MEANING OF "GREAT"

CHAPTER 1

"DO I HAVE A GREAT TEAM CULTURE?"

That's an important question. Let's first think about an unhealthy team culture.

An unhealthy team dynamic makes retention of talent more difficult. The most talented and experienced people with unique skillsets can always easily find other jobs. So if they are unhappy and don't like the tension or stress due to a suboptimal team dynamic, they will soon be gone. This means that you lose the strongest team members, which makes it very difficult to maintain a high-performance team.

"How will I know if I've succeeded in creating a Great Team Culture?" Good question. Here are a few of the significant attributes of a Great Team Culture:

- A Great Team Culture is collaborative.
- A Great Team Culture can withstand difficult times and bounce back fully, quickly.
- A Great Team Culture is one in which *individual* successes are recognized, enjoyed, and appreciated by everyone on the team.
- A Great Team Culture is one in which *team* successes are a cause for celebration.
- A Great Team Culture is one in which every Direct Report values the talents and viewpoints of the other Directs… and every Direct participates in discussions at team meetings.
- A Great Team Culture is one in which the Directs have each other's backs. (Family emergency? Health issue? Vacation? Everyone is

willing to jump in and cover for a teammate... because they know their teammates will do the same for them.)

- A Great Team Culture exceeds expectations consistently.
- A Great Team Culture results in low staff turnover.
- A Great Team Culture is one in which the team is constantly striving to innovate. (No one is satisfied merely with keeping the trains running.)
- A Great Team Culture exists when your Directs are unafraid to challenge you at team meetings and in 1-to-1 meetings.
- A Great Team Culture is a powerful magnet for attracting top talent.

The rest of this book is focused on helping you develop and maintain a Great Team Culture. There is no single silver bullet: a variety of things need to be done in a world-class manner in order to shape a Great Team Culture. *(See Chapter 69: "What's Love Got to Do with It?".)*

CHAPTER 2

GOOD MANAGER VS. GREAT MANAGER –
THE DIFFERENTIATORS

Good Managers help a team to deliver quality results – on time and on budget, while meeting expectations most of the time – and they treat their Direct Reports in a decent manner.

Nothing wrong with that. That can be enough to ensure a company's modest success. But this book is about helping you to become a Great Manager. (If you already are a Great Manager, then parts of this book will be a "refresher" – and you might pick up a technique or two to add to your repertoire.)

"So, what differentiates a Good Manager from a Great Manager?"

The difference is that a Great Manager does everything that a Good Manager does... and also brings these additional value-adds to the table:

- Great Managers create conditions that allow others to succeed. (This is the *most important trait* of a Great Manager.)
- Great managers know what they want their team culture to look like, and they think of themselves as *culture creators.*
- Great Managers work hard to ensure that their Directs are *self*-motivated. *(See "Chapter 57: What Is the One Guaranteed Motivator?")*
- Great Managers think about the training needs of their Direct Reports.
- Great Managers coach their Direct Reports on how to achieve the next step in their careers (even if that results in a top performer leaving their team).

- Great Managers realize that people are different and can think differently about the same set of facts or circumstances. *(See "Chapter 68: Don't Forget the Golden Rule... Revised".)*
- Great Managers use up all their vacation time – and encourage their Direct Reports to do the same. *(See "Chapter 66: Worry-Free Vacations.)*
- Great Managers set context – and then allow their Direct Reports to take ownership of their projects and make decisions.
- Great Managers pose problems to Direct Reports and ask for their suggestions... and listen to the suggestions with full focus.
- Great Managers develop teams that frequently exceed expectations.
- Great Managers do not believe everything they think. Rather, they regularly ask themselves, *"What if I'm wrong?"* You'll be amazed at how much better you become at imagining different scenarios and alternatives when you ask yourself that question. *(See "Chapter 58: "The Difficult Dance of Opposing Principles".)*

These are some of the traits and behaviors that help Great Managers develop a high-performance Great Team Culture.

PART TWO

SOFT SKILLS...
AND A MANAGER'S KEY
RESPONSIBILITY

CHAPTER 3

WHAT TYPES OF SOFT-SKILL MISTAKES IS A MANAGER MOST LIKELY TO MAKE?

"What types of mistakes do recently-hired managers make?"

In short, soft-skill mistakes. Think about soft skills as "human-strategy skills" and "organizational-strategy skills" and "interpersonal skills" and "process skills". The list of possible soft-skill mistakes is long – and each soft-skill mistake can have intricacies and long-term consequences. Some of the most common soft-skill mistakes that managers make are:

- Hiring mistakes
- Meeting-process mistakes
- Triaging mistakes
- Communications mistakes
- Insensitive-action mistakes
- Procedural mistakes
- Making-decisions-with-insufficient-understanding mistakes
- Presentation-style mistakes
- Team-building mistakes
- Leadership mistakes

Yes, the "soft skills" side of the job is where managers most often get into deep doo-doo. Technical mistakes are seldom made by recently-hired managers – because it's fairly easy for a Hiring Manager to vet a managerial candidate's technical skills or industry domain knowledge. Assessing a managerial candidate's soft skills in the interview process is difficult – and it's easy to get it wrong because some candidates are consummate thespians. And even if a managerial candidate is totally genuine during interviews, there are numerous soft skills – and they do not all emerge during an interview loop.

Many managers do not practice soft skills at a world-class level because they have had the least mentoring in them and have had the least training and the least practice in them – so this is the arena in which managers can often "up their game" significantly.

Undoing damage is very hard work and a horrendous waste of time and energy. It can take many months to dig out of a deep hole created in an unthinking moment. It is much smarter, much more efficient, and much less anxiety-producing for managers to learn *how to avoid mistakes* that get them into trouble and to learn *some critical best practices and techniques* that can be implemented proactively.

CHAPTER 4

WHAT IS THE KEY RESPONSIBILITY OF A MANAGER?

You have 5 seconds to respond…

Time is up!

Stumped? Couldn't shout it out instantly?

Answer: Creating conditions that allow others to succeed

Yeah, I know: Different gurus provide different answers to this question… and the answers are all over the map. Some answers are about finances (e.g., meeting revenue and profit-margin projections). Others are about delivering products or services on time and on budget. Others are about beating the competition. Others are about meeting or exceeding sales quotas. Others are about developing lean-and-mean operational capabilities. Others are about innovation. Or people talk in abstractions, such as "being responsible for people/process/products" or "team-building".

The list of managerial responsibilities is long, and each item on the list is important – but none are as important as the critical, essential, core responsibility that a Great Manager has:

Creating conditions that allow others to succeed

"Why?" Because if you succeed in *creating conditions that allow others to succeed*, all of your other managerial responsibilities will fall into place. You will be making optimal use of the people on your team – a requirement for creating a Great Team.

I am *not* saying that you can force your Direct Reports to be successful or guarantee that they will be successful: that is, of course, ultimately *their* job and relies on *their* effort and *their* smarts and *their* experience... *with your support and guidance*. However, you can create conditions that *greatly increase* their chances for success, with the result that your team will perform at a high level and will consistently meet or exceed expectations.

Remember: Developing into a Great Manager requires you to focus on the work-lives of the people on your team. If your Direct Reports succeed, you succeed... and if they fail, you fail.

"How do I create conditions that allow them to succeed?" Keep reading...

CHAPTER 5

CREATING CONDITIONS THAT ALLOW YOUR DIRECT REPORTS TO SUCCEED

You can help your Direct Reports to succeed in a number of ways. For example:

- State your expectations and objectives – verbally, in writing, and repeat as often as necessary.
- Ask your Direct Reports how you might be of help to them. (Keep asking this – at every 1-to-1 meeting – even when a Direct early on says, "I'm fine"... because Directs will be reluctant to ask for help until they really trust their new manager.)
- Remove obstacles preventing Direct Reports from successfully completing a project on time, on budget, and meeting or exceeding expectations.
- Provide skills-enhancement training opportunities for your team.
- Have an open-door policy, which encourages your Directs to drop by your office as often as they feel the need to do so – to get questions answered or to receive a morale booster shot from you or to let you know something.
- Counteract various rumors that upset and distract them.
- Be the buffer between them and the noise coming from other teams and/or upper management.
- Provide the big-picture context of how their efforts contribute to and align with the team's success *and* the company's success. (They

want to know that the work they are doing matters to you, matters to your manager, and matters to the company.)

When you *create conditions that allow your Direct Reports to succeed*, that effort is:

- A *maximize-human-resources* strategy
- A *morale-building* strategy.
- A *develop-people* strategy.

Creating conditions that allow others to succeed is the *unique attribute* that Great Managers possess.

Yes, you read that correctly: I don't want you to become merely a "good" manager – though there's nothing wrong with being a good manager, and the world certainly needs more of them. I want you to become a GREAT MANAGER… and you can only become a Great Manager if you *create conditions that allow others to succeed.*

CHAPTER 6

THE DAY BEFORE YOU START A JOB AS A MANAGER

The moment you walk through the door as the New Manager, people form impressions of you. Yes, instantly. They are scrutinizing everything you do – and don't do – on conscious *and* unconscious levels. They will make immediate judgments. (Think back to your own first sightings of the person who was coming in as *your* new manager.) Yes, the New Manager lives in a glass jar... and everyone is looking in at *you*.

Note: You can skip this chapter if you are not about to step into a new managerial role – but be sure to read it before you begin your next job as a manager.

"Unfair." Yes, it *is* unfair. However, like it or not, that's the reality: at work you exist in a glass jar. People are perception organisms. Before you utter a single word that your Direct Reports can hear and analyze, they will *see* you – how you walk, how you use your hands when talking, how you are dressed, whether you look tired or energetic, what your body type is, where your eyes focus, your interpersonal style. Then, when they hear you utter your first words, they will absorb those words – their literal meaning, their subtext, the body language that accompanies them, and the tone and volume with which they were spoken.

You need to ask yourself is: *"Am I preparing for my first appearance on the scene to ensure that they will perceive me the way I would most like to be perceived?"*

Here are some suggestions on what you can do to optimize the chances that you will be perceived in the way you want to be perceived.

How should you spend the day before your first day on the job? Here's how:

- Relax!
- Do something enjoyable.
- Do *not* spend the day prepping for your first day. (Do that in preceding days, if necessary – but *not* the day before your first day on the job.)
- Get a good night's sleep... so that you show up that first day feeling refreshed, looking rested, and feeling and appearing confident.
- Have a good breakfast.

"Why? Does it really matter? Shouldn't I be preparing for my first day at work?"

Yes, it *really* matters. No, you should *not* be preparing for your first day at work on the day before your first day on the new job; do that in the previous week. Your sole preparation is to get into the best physical and mental shape possible.

Tip: Being well-rested, looking confident, and being 100% alert optimizes your chance of making a Great First Impression.

What will their brains register when you first appear? Here's a short list:

- Do you look energetic? Or worn? Pale from exhaustion? Bags under your eyes?
- Do you exude calm and confidence? Or are you perceived as tense and nervous?
- Do you seem self-absorbed or dazed? Or do people experience you as inclusive and relational?
- Do you seem robotic? Or are you perceived as an accessible human?
- Do you make eye contact? Or do people think you're avoiding them?
- Do you greet everyone with a relaxed, friendly, and unrushed "Hello"?

- Do you smile easily, comfortably, warmly? (Not a practiced "professional smile"… but a real smile.)
- Are you able respond to questions and greetings with grace, interpersonal skill, and full focus?
- Do you chuckle or laugh when something humorous is said?

First impressions are not erased or forgotten quickly by those who are watching your every move – so be sure that the first impression that you make is the one that you want to make.

CHAPTER 7

WEEKLY "MANDATORY ACTIVITIES"

(If You've Recently Stepped into a Manager Role)

Appendices 1-4 contain four tables with recommended "mandatory activities" for the first 4 weeks on the new job. The recommendations address activities that many New Managers do *not* do (but should do) in their first 4 weeks on the job – to maximize their chances of long-term success.

> **Note:** If you've been in your managerial role for a while, the "Mandatory Activities" tables in the *Appendices* might not apply to you. However, even if you've been in your managerial role for longer than 4 weeks, you might look over the tables anyways – just in case there is an activity that you have not done and might still benefit from doing.

The recommendations in the tables are there to *pull you out of the daily humdrum* so that you can step back and think big-picture about how to strategically view your activities in order to maximize the chances of your team's success (which, of course, is also *your* success).

Managers constantly find themselves in unique situations. Ergo, I can't say with certainty which "mandatory" activities are truly mandatory or fit the realities that a particular manager lands in. You might decide that an activity listed in Week 2 might be better to do in Week 1 or in Week 4... or Week 10. You might also decide that some activities might not be appropriate for your situation at all. The tables in the *Appendices* are there as reminders of soft-skill strategies that can make you and your team more successful.

Note: You're the manager, so part of your job – every day – is figuring out what's relevant and what isn't... and prioritizing appropriately. So consider the Mandatory Activities as a check-list of activities that managers often overlook and which you should consider doing – because, in most cases, they will make you a more effective manager... and lead you further along the path to being a Great Manager.

PART THREE

EVERY MEETING COUNTS

CHAPTER 8

YOUR FIRST TEAM "GATHERING"

(Not a Meeting)

Yes, I said "team *gathering*". You want this first get-together with your new team to be easy-going and light-hearted and human-oriented: a meet-and-greet of sorts, an ice-breaker – *not* a business meeting. This sends an important signal to your team about the culture you intend to create.

The "Self-Intro Cheat-Sheet" exercise *(see template, below)* has always been enjoyable and relaxing when I've conducted it – and you will likely see smiles and hear laughter. It's a great way to kick off your tenure as their manager. And the key message to your team is: "This manager is interested in us as people. Yeah, we'll work hard, but we also will have fun." And you will... and they will.

So devote your first team gathering solely to this self-introduction exercise. Make photocopies of the "Self-Intro Cheat Sheet". At the start of the meeting explain what's going to happen – and then pass out the Crib Sheets. Jump around the table, calling on people in a random fashion, which keeps everyone alert.

Have fun!

Best Practice: Some of your Direct Reports might be a bit nervous about this activity, so it's very important that you explain that this is a self-introduction ice-breaker – and that *you will go first*. That will set the tone: if you're revealing, they will be, too. If you are straightforward, they will be, too. If you have a sense of humor about your past, they will, too.

Note: If you have been on this team as a sole contributor and then have been promoted to manager, this exercise might be unnecessary if your Direct Reports already know each other really well and you know them really well.

That said, even people who have worked together for a while will be surprised (and often delighted) by some new factoids they learn about their teammates.

Self-Intro "Cheat Sheet"

- Your name
- The city you were born in
- The city (or cities) you grew up in
- The places you lived in as an adult
- The first job that you had
- The weirdest job you have ever had
- The job you had before coming to this company
- How long you worked at that company
- How long you have worked at this company
- Your role(s) at this company
- Your favorite food dish or favorite cuisine
- Your favorite non-work activity or hobby (only legal and non-intimate activities)
- What you want to be doing 10 years from now

CHAPTER 9

THREE TEAM-MEETING FUNDAMENTALS

1. **Team Meeting ownership** – You own the scheduling, agenda, and arrangements for the weekly recurring team meetings.

2. **Length and frequency of team meetings** – Team meetings should be scheduled for 1 hour and should occur weekly.

   a. If the agenda is short, you can end the meeting before the hour is up (but I guarantee you that this will seldom happen).

   b. If you know that one of the topics is complex and could by itself use up 30-60 minutes, schedule a separate meeting for that one topic.

3. **Team meetings are sacrosanct** – Team meetings establish a "rhythm of the business" and are key in creating a Great Team Culture. This is where great collaborative problem-solving can occur. This is where you model the behaviors you expect from your team.

Important: Every member of your team needs to get a loud and clear message from you that *meetings matter* and that you expect everyone to be on time and to participate.

Caveat: You should rarely cancel the weekly team meetings. If you have to cancel a team meeting, try to reschedule and hold the meeting within 48 hours.

CHAPTER 10

How to Run Effective Team Meetings

Facilitating great team meetings requires great technique, a tried-and-proven protocol, and some artistry.

If you do your meeting-prep homework, punctual attendance will not be a problem. Au contraire, your Direct Reports will look forward to team meetings and will show up on time, every time!

Best Practices for Facilitating Team Meetings

Each of your Direct Reports will appreciate an efficiently-run and useful meeting. They – like you – have a lot on their plates, and they don't want to sit through boring meetings that are a waste of their time. You don't want that either!

When every one of your team meetings starts on time, and every Direct Report is there on time, and everyone looks forward to productive team meetings, and you keep people on topic and move through the agenda effortlessly and efficiently, you will be on your way to creating a Great Team Culture.

The body language of your Directs will instantly inform you of whether they think the meetings you run are worthwhile – and their degree of participation will be another obvious clue to whether you have succeeded in creating useful and informative meetings.

Warning: Gobs of time can be wasted when team meetings regularly start late or if some Directs keep showing up late. When meetings start late because certain individuals show up late, the team loses time that it can never get back – and it's also psychologically disruptive. Don't let this happen! Not only is time lost, but the morale hit is significant.

Serious Mistakes in Facilitating Team Meetings

Some managers dominate the team meeting by talking almost the entire time – in effect, lecturing – with little or no team-member participation.

Yes, there *are* times when a manager needs to convey information about a new company strategy or a new H.R. policy or a new urgency. In such cases, the manager is going to need time to transfer necessary information – but even then, the manager should build in sufficient time for questions and discussions. That said, the best team meetings are ones in which the manager (you!) blabs very little and provides a lot of verbal space for team members.

Here are few terrible traits that I've seen exhibited by managers when facilitating team meetings:

- Calling on one or two people way more than you call on other team members.
- Cutting off team members before they've finished making their point.
- Coming to the team meeting unprepared for discussing key topics.
- Lecturing instead of engaging team members.
- Criticizing one or two Direct Reports in front of all the other Directs.
- Getting argumentative when challenged by your Directs.
- Giving your opinion before you ask your Directs for their opinions. (It's OK to give your opinion *after* you've elicited their opinions.)
- Asking for input from your Directs when you've already made up your mind.

Worst Practice: Talking too much. (The less you talk, the better.)

Lousy Ways to Present an Agenda to the Team

Agendas are important. Many managers think that agendas are trivial or that they are too busy to "waste time" creating thoughtful, well-planned agendas *with input from the team*. Such thinking is a serious mistake. Well-thought-out agendas and skillful facilitation are the foundation of productive team meetings.

Here is a list of some of the worst "agenda" practices by managers, each of which I have witnessed numerous times over the years:

- Manager prepares no agenda.
- Manager walks in and verbally ad-libs an agenda (which usually doesn't "hold" for the length of the team meeting).
- Manager walks in and writes an agenda on the whiteboard (which usually doesn't "hold" for the length of the team meeting).
- Manager sends out an agenda 12-24 hours before the meeting... and then does not follow the agenda.
- Manager never requests agenda items from team members a day or two before the meeting.
- Manager never asks the team, at the start of a team meeting, if they have additional agenda items.
- Manager does not prioritize items on the agenda – and then skips around from topic to topic in a random, ad-libbed manner.

Because you are striving to become or continue being a Great Manager, I know that you will never commit any of these sins. *Right?*

So, how should a manager handle agenda preparation? Read on...

Agenda Preparation

Team meetings have various purposes – and usually contain a combination of purposes: e.g., information sharing, group problem-solving, discussing opportunities for new products and services, announcing changes in company policy or mission, and so forth.

Prepare a *draft* team-meeting Agenda of topics that you think the team needs to discuss. Include the following types of items:

- Making announcements of things you need to communicate to your team.
- Revisiting a topic that was discussed weeks or months before – and that still needs resolution.
- Discussion of ongoing projects.
- Discussion of new projects.
- Discussion of a problem that requires group-think to solve.

  Tip: If one of the topics requires a long discussion (say, more than 30 minutes), it won't leave much time for the other items on the agenda. Rather than rushing through the agenda and trying to squeeze all the topics into the 1-hour team meeting, consider organizing a separate meeting dedicated to that topic.

- Send the draft Agenda to your Direct Reports *the day before* the team meeting, and ask them if they have any items they would like to add.

Great Agenda Format for Team Meetings

Great Teams have Great Team Meetings… and Great Team Meetings require Great Agendas. Using a time-tested Agenda format will allow you to facilitate team meetings in an optimal manner… which is a deeply satisfying experience for the team and for you.

Here are some reasons why the time-tested Agenda format that I recommend *(see Agenda sample, below)* is effective in ensuring productive team meetings:

- If you prepare the Agenda the day before the team meeting, the following benefits accrue:
  - Your Direct Reports have time to absorb what's going to be discussed (transparency), and they will arrive at the meeting intellectually and emotionally prepared to march through the Agenda.

- ○ Your Directs have the opportunity to send you additional Agenda topics, and you will have time to prioritize them and reserve minutes to discuss them.
- Having a column titled "Presenter of Issue" makes your Directs aware of who is getting their name in lights… and makes them more eager to make their realities known to you and to the team *by contributing* to the agenda preparation.
- Having a column titled "Time (min.)" gives your team a sense of how much time you want to be dedicated to each topic… and if, at the start of the meeting, someone wants to add an Agenda item, everyone can see and discuss the time-and-topic triage that needs to occur.
- The "Action Items" section is where to park "next steps" that have been raised at the meeting… so such items are not "lost" and will be followed up on at the next meeting.

AGENDA *<sample>*

23 October 2045

Item	Presenter of Issue	Time (min.)
Announcements? (60 seconds or less)	All	3 min
Additional agenda items?	All	2 min
H.R. policy change	<you>	3 min
Marketing plans for product roll-out	Susan	10 min
Status of miracle feature development	Paul	10 min.
Vendor budget status? new Vendor needs?	All	5 min
SolveAll tool: do we want to pilot?	Richard	5 min.
IP Roadmap – next assignments	Jack/All	10 min.
Plan for authoring content going forward	Anne	10 min.
Mid-Year Review (dates for)	<you>	2 min.

Action Items

Name	Item	Date Due	Date Done	Done
Richard	Further assess SolveAll tool to make a go/no-go decision re piloting	6/23		
Susan	Reserve conference rooms for Train-the-Trainer sessions and send out invitations	6/25		
Paul	Schedule review for miracle feature	6/25		

| All | Provide vacation plans for next 6 months (days out of the office and not online) | 6/28 | | |
| <you> | Team coverage worldwide for next 6 months of vacations and holidays | 7/01 | | |

Truly an Open-Ended Discussion?

Be clear about your intention when you place an item on the Agenda for discussion. If you don't want to discuss an item, don't put it on the Agenda... or simply announce the decision that you've made and why you made it – without inviting discussion.

If there's a reaction – say, a couple of Directs have questions about what you just announced – then you of course respond to the questions.

- Do *not* pretend that you want input from your Direct Reports or your peers when you've already made your decision.
- Don't be a coward. If you've made up your mind about something, put it out there in a straightforward manner... and be brave enough to deal with the reactions. You're not fooling anyone if you've made up your mind but pretend that you haven't – and if you pretend you're looking for input from your team when what you really are trying to do is get their buy-in by coercing them into agreeing with you. You think it's subtle: it is *not* subtle.
- Faking indecision and open-mindedness will be perceived as highly manipulative, sleazy, and dishonest.

Don't Opine First (or: How *Not* to Shut Down Team Discussions)

If you want input – open-hearted, open-minded, and uncensored input – from your Direct Reports, do not raise a topic for discussion and then give your opinion right off the bat. You will learn more if you wait to hear from your team... and the resulting discussion will be much better – more interesting and livelier.

If you want to dampen a discussion before it starts, the best way to do that is to open your mouth first. I have seen many managers – even veteran managers – commit this error again and again... and then they wonder why no one is speaking up. The answers are simple:

- They do not speak up because they are *scared to disagree* because they don't know how their manager will respond.
- They do not speak up because they worry about whether there will be retribution if they disagree publicly.
- They do not speak up because their "read" on the situation is that manager has already decided what to do... so why bother?

If you want the best and most-creative thinking from your Directs, simply raise the topic or frame the issue... and then turn to the team and say: "So, what do you think?" or "How should we handle this?" or "Any suggestions on how to proceed?" And then lean back in your chair and await the barrage of brilliant, analytic, and out-of-the-box thinking. You'll enjoy watching your team rise to the occasion!

If, however, you put your thumb on the scale by telling your Direct Reports what you want to do before they've had a chance to think or a chance to talk, you're not going to get much useful feedback. And the meeting will be boring, awkward, and tense.

Note: Once you've had a few months to create a Great Team Culture, your Direct Reports won't be afraid to speak up or contradict you... even if you slip up and begin a discussion by disclosing your point of view at the outset.

However, until you have successfully established a Great Team Culture, your Directs will tend to lean back and watch which way the wind is blowing.

"How Do I Ensure that the Best and Most Creative Thinking Bubbles Up?"

As the manager and facilitator of your meeting, it is your responsibility to ensure that the best ideas make it to the table. You can make that happen by creating a culture in which it is clear to everyone that everyone is expected to participate.

"Why is it so important to set the expectation of participation?" Because that is how you will get the highest IQ and maximum innovation from your team... and that is one way to improve morale and create a Great Team Culture. It is not unusual to have one or two people dominate team discussions due to sheer force of personality, due to their being fast on their feet, due to their being narcissists, due to their being more senior or more knowledgeable than most of the team members, or due to their having little impulse control.

Best Practice: Do *not* let dominators dominate your team meetings – because others on the team will withdraw and contribute less to the discussion than they would have otherwise (and perhaps start looking for another job because they sense that you won't have control of your team or you won't have their backs).

Remember: It is sometimes true (but not always true) that most of the good ideas come from a few people on your team. However, people who are shy or less quick to talk might actually have a super-great idea – and you'll never hear their ideas because they lack confidence or because they want to avoid verbal fisticuffs. *(See the next two sections in this chapter: "How Do I Ensure that Everyone Participates Equally?" and "How Do I Deal with Ultra-Aggressive Talkers?")*

Note: Males dominate conversations more often than females do, so keep an eye out for gender differences – and then do something constructive (and subtle) about it. *(Again, see the next two sections.)*

Note: Keep an eye out for cultural differences. E .g., people from Texas or New York City or Italy or Greece are more likely to shout out – and people from Minnesota or Vermont or Cambodia or Japan are more likely to sit attentively and respectfully. (Yes, I realize that I might just have set off shock waves on the politically-incorrect seismic scale. Such generalizations are awful – and accurate only some of the time. I know that I should avoid such generalizations, but sometimes…)

"How Do I Ensure that Everyone Participates Equally?"

It's important to lay out some "ground rules" about how you expect your Direct Reports to behave at team meetings. Do this at the start of your first couple of team meetings… and then repeat whenever a new Direct joins your team. If team behavior backslides, you might need to vocalize a reminder every 3-4 months. Sometimes, however you have a tense situation that is not resolved by spelling out "ground rules" (good behaviors that you expect) – and in such cases, more forceful techniques are required.

A simple technique – the Seating Chart Technique – will help you control those who tend to dominate discussions. The technique also ensures that those who tend to sit quietly or passively during discussions are drawn out of their shell and included.

The Seating Chart Technique

I have used the Seating Chart technique over the years, and it works like a charm.

- When the team convenes, make a quick Seating Chart, and then…
  - When someone speaks, you put a check-mark (√) by that person's name. Do *not* call on or respond to that person again until you call on those who have not spoken yet.
- If dominant types interrupt you or a team member to state their opinion a second time, do *not* respond to the person. Instead, turn to one of the people on your team who speak up less often – and say something like, "So, what do you think of that suggestion?"

And then repeat that with one or two more of the people who seldom speak up.

This tactic has the dual effect of putting the brakes on the aggressive talkers and simultaneously letting the quieter ones know that they can't hide out.

- o This can defuse aggressive types who like to go head-to-head with their manager and who often think that the rest of the team members always agree with them.
- o The team dynamic changes for the better – in wondrous and unexpected ways – when team members do not always agree with the aggressive types.

Note: By the end of the team meeting, every member of your team will have participated a nearly equal number of times (say, within one check-mark of each other). They will have learned that you are inclusive and that you want to hear everyone's ideas and reactions. You have telegraphed the strong messages that non-participation is not an option and that dominating team meetings is not OK. *(See the next heading, "How Do I Deal with Ultra-Aggressive Talkers?")*

"How Do I Deal with Ultra-Aggressive Talkers?" (Who Dominate Team Meetings and Often Try to Change the Subject)

If the Seating Chart Technique discussed in the previous section does not succeed in controlling ultra-aggressive talkers, here are two additional techniques for dealing with out-of-control talkers – and ensuring that the less-talkative Direct Reports speak up.

The Poker Chip Game

The "Poker Chip Game" should be reserved for extreme situations – i.e., if the Seating Chart Technique discussed in the previous sections doesn't work.

The Poker Chip Game is a heavy-handed technique, but it is very effective for two reasons:

- It creates a game-like atmosphere, and people enjoy the game (except perhaps for the Ultra-Aggressive Talkers, who feel constrained).
- The poker chips become the referee, rather than you, which relieves you of the unpleasant duty of being the enforcer – because the chips act as very visible hard data that is difficult for your Ultra-Aggressive Talkers and your other Direct Reports to ignore. Truly, the chips don't lie.

You need to have poker chips – two for each member of your team. (The color of the chips doesn't matter.) *Before* you pass out the poker chips, explain to your team that the "Poker Chip Game" is designed to encourage participation from all team members. (Yes, be very transparent about why you're using this technique. No one will mistake your intent.)

When you've completed your introduction, spell out the rules of the game:

- "Each of you gets two poker chips."
- "When you speak up, you toss one poker chip into the center of the table."
- "When you have used up your two chips, you are *not* allowed to speak again until everyone else has used up their two chips."
- "Those people who have not used up their chips must speak up on the topic at hand until they have used up their two chips."
- "When all the chips are in the center of the table, they will be redistributed."

Now pass out two poker chips to each Direct Report... and let the game begin.

Note: When your team becomes well-behaved and the Great Team Culture has taken hold, you can of course choose to suspend the Poker Chip Game – but don't be surprised if your Directs resist giving it up.

Re-directional Phrases

You need to have at your command a "vocabulary" for responding to ultra-aggressive talkers. Here are a few examples of phrases that you can use to artfully deal with people who have a tendency to interrupt or change the subject or who speak up too often:

If the Ultra-Aggressive Talker's interruption or comment pertains to the topic under discussion:

- "I want to let <so-and-so> finish what s-he was saying."
- "I understand your concern."
- Turn to everyone around the table (making eye contact with each individual), and say: "I want to hear from everyone about <the aggressor's> comment."

If the Ultra-Aggressive Talker tries to change the subject:

- "We can try to address that later, but we need to stay focused on this topic until we reach a resolution."
- "I'll add that to the Agenda, and we'll address it later if there is time."
- "You're clearly passionate about that topic. If we don't have time to address this in today's meeting, we can try to address it in email – or I'll add the topic to next week's Agenda."

These types of *re-directional phrases* send a clear message to the Ultra-Aggressors Talker that certain behaviors are not welcomed and are not tolerated – and that you can't be bamboozled or cowed. That powerful message is equally (or even more) important to the other members of your team, who do not appreciate the disruptions and tensions caused by the Ultra-Aggressive Talker – and who will be grateful that you are keeping the dominant types under control.

Remember: A well-thought-out Agenda creates a framework that most of your team will adhere to (because they *contributed* to shaping the Agenda). It also makes it easy for everyone to notice the "disrupting influences", which *dis-empowers* the Ultra-Aggressive Talker – often faster than you would have guessed – because the Ultra-Aggressive

Talker is exposed and becomes aware that all eyes are on her/him. *(See the Chapter 10 sections, "Agenda Preparation", "Great Agenda Format for Team Meetings", and "Agenda <sample>".)*

Amazing – You Reap What You Sow

Over the years I have seen, time and again, that when I facilitated team meetings in a way that was all-inclusive, a *new culture was created* by the third or fourth meeting. The meetings then became extraordinarily collaborative, with people bouncing off each other's ideas and generating a lot of energy. Even the initially-reluctant-to-speak people started speaking up – sometimes to a surprising degree.

You'll be amazed, perhaps even shocked, when you see this happen. It happens because your Direct Reports feel encouraged and empowered by you – because you have their back – and because you have set a high bar for participation (and have been able, in a nice way, to keep the Ultra-Aggressive Talkers under control). In addition, the reticent team members start saying to themselves, *"I better speak up when I have a good thought. That's better than keeping quiet and being called on when I don't have much to say."*

You'll feel great when everyone participates fully at your team meetings. And it will serve as evidence that you are on the road that takes you from being a Good Manager to becoming a Great Manager. *(See Chapter 2, "Good Manager vs. Great Manager – the Differentiators".)*

CHAPTER 11

YOUR *FIRST* 1-TO-1 MEETING WITH *YOUR* MANAGER

Don't be casual about preparing for your first 1-to-1 meeting with your manager. This first 1-to-1 can set the tone (in your manager's mind) for the relationship for months to come. You want your manager to believe that you understand the big picture and also are attentive to detail.

Do the following things the day before you meet (so you have time to mull over and rethink what you would like to accomplish at this first meeting):

- Prepare an Agenda. *(Use the Agenda format provided in the previous chapter.)*
- Think about the things that make you nervous – and see if that makes you think of questions you would like to ask (whose answers will reduce your anxiety level).
- Think about whether there are H.R. policies that you're unclear about.
- Get clarifications about schedules and upcoming deadlines.
- Ask about expectations – and how success will be measured.
- Ask about upcoming unit-wide, division-wide, and company-wide meetings so that you can get these on your calendar immediately (to avoid conflicts with other appointments you want to make and to reschedule team meetings, interview loops, and 1-to-1's as necessary).

What Are Your Manager's Concerns and Priorities?

You need to know what's top-of-mind for your manager – so ask. Here are some things you need to know to best understand your manager's view of the work-related realities:

- Find out which projects or situations (other than yours) are your manager's Priority 1's.
- Find out who your manager's peers are.
- Find out which units your manager works with most closely.

What Are Your *Skip-Level* Manager's Concerns and Priorities?

Ask your manager about the concerns and priorities of your skip-level manager (i.e., your manager's manager). Some of these might or might not be the same as those of your manager... though usually there is a significant overlap or at least some alignment.

Make a mental note of any non-overlap or non-alignment between the goals of your manager and your skip-level manager – because these probably matter a lot to your skip-level manager. Perhaps they represent a stretch goal or opportunity for you. Perhaps they are a secret strategy that your skip-level manager hopes will catapult her/him up the corporate ladder. Perhaps they are indicative of a strong passion. Whatever the case, you will be greatly appreciated if you can make any contributions to your skip-level manager's non-overlap goals (while, of course, accomplishing the goals that you and your manager have agreed on).

Caution: Before helping your skip-level manager, be certain that your manager and skip-level manager are in synch and get along well. If you sense that your manager is not enthused about your skip-level manager, do not help your skip-level manager unless directed to do so by your manager.

What Does Your Manager Most Want You to Accomplish in the First 3 Months on the Job?

You need to know which issues fall into which categories for your manager:

- Critical issues – must get to work on right away and complete ASAP
- Important issues – must do within a reasonable time frame
- Nice-to-haves – if there's time (ha!)

Remember: Be sure you leave this first 1-to-1 meeting with your manager with a clear understanding of what's top-of-mind for your manager.

Tip: If everything is a priority, then nothing is a priority. That's why you need a *prioritized* list from your manager (not merely a laundry list) of what s-he expects you to accomplish.

Warning: If you've had a mess dropped into your lap, see *"Part Four: Triaging Your Way Out of a Mess"*.

Who Did *Not* Get the Job? (a Dicey Topic to Bring Up)

Who else wanted the job you got? If there were internal candidates who now report to you or with whom you had peer relationships in the past or who will be a peer of yours now, you need to be aware of possible residual tension and unhappiness… and then figure out whether there is anything that you can do proactively to lessen the tension (rather than waiting for a blow-up) – because potential eruptions and invisible fissures will be all around you.

Here are some things that would be good to know:

- Who were the other candidates for the position you have?

  Warning: Probably best to not ask about this at your first 1-to-1 with your manager. You need to figure out whether and when to ask your manager about this. (You might learn what you want to know from the grapevine… but that info might trickle in over the months.)

- If one of the candidates is someone who is on your team and now reports to you, you'll have to figure out how to talk to this person about the situation as you consider and learn the following from your manager:
  - Do other teammates (your Direct Reports) know that this person applied for and didn't get your job?
  - Is the person still looking for/applying for other management positions? If 'yes', assure the person that this will not be held against her/him.
  - Has this person been a manager before? If 'yes', and if you've never before been a manager before, it might be an especially bitter pill for the losing candidate to swallow.
  - Do your other Directs (this person's peers) like the losing candidate? If they do like and respect the person, then they might not appreciate your arrival on the scene.
  - Do your other Directs *not* like and respect the losing candidate? See what you can learn about that *without asking*.
- How did your manager present the news to the disappointed internal candidate? (This is important… and you'll learn much about the situation and about what your manager is like – but you can't force this information-gathering with your manager… because s-he could be feeling shaky or upset or uncomfortable about the decision to hire you instead of the internal candidate.)
- If the person is an internal candidate who is not on your team, but is a person your team and/or you will be working with, you need to be sensitive in your first meetings with such a person.

Remember: The candidate may harbor a "why-did-they-hire-you?"attitude that is never said aloud, and which can result in unpleasant and unhelpful undercurrents. You need to try extra hard to develop a reasonably good working relationship with the candidate who did not get the job.

CHAPTER 12

YOUR *FIRST* 1-TO-1 MEETING WITH EACH OF YOUR DIRECT REPORTS

Schedule a 1.5-hour meeting with each of your new Direct Reports for that critical initial 1-to-1 meeting. Yes, you read that right: one-point-five-hour meeting. There will be lots to talk about as you get to know each other... and you can always end early. What you do not want to happen is for your Directs to feel that you're rushing and that you're pushing them out of your office before the conversation comes to a natural end.

Caveat: *Do not gamble the future by rushing the present.* Do not rush this first meeting... because it will set the tone and lay the foundation for your future relationship.

Note: For guidelines on future, weekly, recurring 1-to-1 meetings with your Direct Reports, see *"Chapter 13: The Art of Recurring 1-to-1 Meetings with your Direct Reports"*.

You want each of your Directs to leave that first 1-to-1 meeting feeling good, really good. Specifically, you want your Directs to feel that:

- You care about them as people.
- You care about them as sole contributors.
- You care about them as team members.
- You care about their career goals.

- They have gotten a sense of who you are – and realize that they are lucky to have a thoughtful and mature adult as their new manager.

If you succeed on these five counts at this first 1-to-1 with each of your Direct Reports, you'll be off to a great start.

You can, of course, go with the flow of the conversation rather than follow the script line by line and point by point. That said, the script *(see Agenda Format, below)* covers a lot of important territory.

Note: This will be the first and last 1-to-1 meeting with your Directs that you own and facilitate. Future 1-to-1's will be owned by each of your Direct Reports. It's *their* meeting. It's their responsibility to come prepared… and they understand (because you will tell them at the end of this first 1-to-1 – and then repeat this at a team meeting) that the purpose of the weekly recurring 1-to-1 meeting is to address *their* concerns.

Agenda for the *Initial* 1-to-1 Meeting with Each Direct Report

Below is the template to use for your *first* 1-to-1 with each of your Direct Reports. You will facilitate this initial 1-to-1 meeting. (Future 1-to-1's are owned by your Directs, and they will facilitate the recurring 1-to-1 meetings that they have with you.)

Best Practice: Take *handwritten* notes directly on the hard-copy print-out. The sound of keys being tapped introduces a *mechanical* element to the meeting – and this is not conducive to creating the *personal* tone that you want for this first 1-to-1.

Agenda Format for *Initial* 1-to-1 Meeting with Each Direct Report

Name: _____

Date: _____

Time: _____

Goal: Learn about the person

1. How long have you worked here?
2. What were you doing before you took a job at this company?
   <skip the question if the person's current job is their first job >
   a. What was the best thing about that job?
   b. What was the worst thing about that job?
3. What is the most rewarding thing about your current (or most recent) job?
4. What is the most difficult or frustrating thing about your current job?
5. What motivates you?
6. How do you like to be recognized and rewarded?
7. How can I help you be successful?
8. What do you want to be doing 5 years from now?

Goal: Learn about the team and its history

<assumes your team existed before you were hired; skip these questions – or recast them – if this is a newly-formed team; make clear that you are not asking them to "name names"; the focus is on "team">

1. How would you describe this team in a concise way? (think: elevator-pitch)
2. What do you consider the special strengths of this team?
3. In what areas does the team have room for improvement, areas that need to be worked on?

4. How would you describe the team's culture?

Goal: Learn about the customers/dependencies

1. What teams or people do you interact with, internally and externally?
    a. What's going well?
    b. What is not going well?
    c. What would you like to see change in those interactions?
2. Do you have the equipment, supplies, applications, and tools to get the job done optimally?

Goal: Find out what *they* want to know

1. Is there anything else that you would like me to know about you, your work, etc. that we haven't already covered?
2. What would you like to know about me?
3. If you were in my shoes, what would you focus on *first*?
4. What is the *second* area that you would focus on?
5. What is the *third* area that you would focus on?

CHAPTER 13

THE ART OF RECURRING 1-TO-1 MEETINGS WITH YOUR DIRECT REPORTS

O ne of the most common complaints heard from Direct Reports is: *"I don't get enough face-time with my manager."*

I've heard that complaint from all kinds of people – e.g., from high-maintenance types, from ambitious types, and from stellar team-member types. It doesn't matter what the nature of the need is – the need is there. It's easiest to address the need proactively by having weekly 1-to-1 meetings with each of your Direct Reports.

Remember: Face-time with their manager is incredibly important to Direct Reports. Never underestimate this – and never forget this. They want to feel that their manager knows about and cares about what they are going through – both accomplishments and challenges.

Best Practice: Never cancel a 1-to-1 without immediately scheduling a make-up.

Tip: If you prefer to not have weekly 1-hour 1-to-1's, remember that it's better to have a weekly 1-to-1 meeting for 30 minutes than to have a 1-to-1 meeting every other week for 60 minutes.

Worst Practice: Making your office the location of bad news. Your office should be a haven for any of your Direct Reports to enter at any time. That won't be the case if 80% of the time you deliver bad news or negative feedback when people are in your office.

Benefits for Direct Reports

When Direct Reports own their 1-to-1 meetings with you, it's a good thing because it gives them the:

- Opportunity to give their manager a progress report on project schedules.
- Opportunity to give their manager a head's-up about an upcoming issue.
- Opportunity to ask their manager for feedback on various matters.
- Opportunity to demonstrate their competence to their manager.
- Opportunity to discuss career ambitions (if they choose to bring up that topic).
- Opportunity to discuss skill-sets and desired training.
- Opportunity to develop/improve meeting-facilitation skills.

Why Career Discussions Are Important

I always wanted my managers to care about me, to assist me in my career aspirations. Over the years, as a manager, I've found that to be almost universally true of all the people who have been on my teams. Almost all employees, in secret or transparently, think about "next steps" in their careers. So your Direct Reports can do this *with* your help and encouragement – or *without* your help and encouragement. Which is preferable? That's a no-brainer. If you help your Directs with their career goals, they will appreciate you and feel loyal to you and to the team – and as long as they are on the team, they will go the extra mile for you and for their teammates.

Direct Reports are often reluctant to discuss career ambitions (especially during, say, the first six months of your tenure) because they fear that any discussion of "moving on" or "change in career desires" will result in their manager penalizing them in some way. So don't push hard on this. You can make it known – at team meetings is best as well as in 1-to-1's – that you're happy to discuss their career plans with them, that you understand that people move around and that's part of life – and you can even tell them about some of your past career moves.

It's a "trust" thing… and trust develops slowly in most people. They will let you know when they trust you enough to discuss their future career desires – and they will do that only if you let them know that you are open to doing that… and only when they believe that there is no downside, no punishment for disloyalty, for divulging their "other" desires.

Best Practice: Initiate a career-development conversation twice a year. Don't schedule such meetings with your Direct Reports until you feel certain that a level of trust has developed… which could take 3-6 months. When the trust level is evident, tell your team – at a team meeting – that you're going to schedule a ½-hour meeting with each of them to discuss skills development and career paths.

Some of your Directs will welcome such a conversation, and some will be nervous. You'll know which is which – unless you're so anxious about having such conversations that you're not picking up on their signals: tone of voice… eye contact… fidgeting… foot tapping… finger tapping… leaning away from you as they sit… glancing at their watch… shuffling papers… shaky voice.

Gut-Check: The profound question for you is: "Are *you* comfortable talking with your Direct Reports about career plans that might have zero to do with you, your team, or your company?"

If you are not comfortable with such conversations, then do not invite such conversations… because your Directs will feel misled and betrayed if you talk the talk, but don't walk the walk. (Get some coaching/ mentoring from an experienced manager, who can give you pointers about how to discuss career ambitions with your Directs.)

Benefits for the Manager (that's You!)

Having weekly recurring 1-to-1's with each of your Direct Reports benefits you as well:

- Helps build a solid relationship with each of your Directs.
- Keeps you up-to-date on your Directs' state of mind.
- Gives you the opportunity to get to know your Direct better.
- Allows you to mentor/coach your Directs.

Best Practice: A career-discussion meeting should be a set-in-stone topic twice a year – but make this a separate 1-hour meeting (rather than using the regular 1-to-1 time slot).

Agenda for *Recurring* 1-to-1 Meetings with Each Direct Report

Below is a template for your Direct Reports to use for their recurring (weekly) 1-to-1 meetings with you.

Each of your Direct Reports is responsible for filling out the 1-to-1 form and bringing *two copies* to the meeting – one for them, and one for you.

Remember: You do *not* facilitate recurring 1-to-1 meetings. It is *their* meeting: they *own* it. It's their time with you – not your time with them.

Letting them facilitate the meeting provides them with practice in creating an agenda, prioritizing topics, estimating how much time is needed per topic, and so forth – which is excellent preparation for them in learning how to conduct a meeting… and perhaps becoming a manager one day.

If you need time to discuss a a topic of your own during their 1-to-1 meeting, let your Direct Reports know that at the beginning of the meeting: e.g., "I'll need 10 minutes at the end of the meeting to discuss xyz." That gives your Directs a head's-up in case they want to adjust their 1-to-1 Agenda to create space for your topic. If that's problematic, set up a separate meeting to discuss your topic with them.

Tip: Some meetings fall into a special category – e.g., promotion or bonus meetings and performance-review meetings. For such special discussions, you need to schedule a separate meeting. Do *not* use your Directs' weekly 1-to-1 meetings for your purposes. (Don't forget: The 1-to-1 meetings are *their* meetings.)

1-to-1 Meeting – <date>

_____

<name of Direct Report>

Red flags *(needs immediate attention of or intervention by your Manager)*
-

Yellow flags *(FYI or "heads-up" for your Manager)*
-

Calendar commitments for next 30-45 days
[significant meetings (such as Project Checkpoint / Milestone Reviews), trips, vacations]

Date   Activity

Commitments, Special Projects
-
-

Progress Towards Deliverables, Commitments & Personal Development Goals
-
-

The Good
-
-

The Bad

-
-

The Undecided

-
-

Other Discussion Points

-
-

Personal 'happiness' scale of 1-100

(1 being bad beyond words, 100 being near-impossible-to-reach happiness)

1 — 10 — 20 — 30 — 40 — 50 — 60 — 70 — 80 — 90 — 100
<comment to explain up/down change in rating>

Team's 'happiness' scale of 1-100 (Direct Report's perception of team dynamic)

(1 being bad beyond words, 100 being near-impossible-to-reach happiness)

1 — 10 — 20 — 30 — 40 — 50 — 60 — 70 — 80 — 90 — 100
<comment to explain up/down change in rating>

PART FOUR

TRIAGING YOUR WAY
OUT OF A MESS

WHAT IF YOU LEARN DURING THE FIRST WEEK ON THE JOB THAT YOU'VE BEEN DROPPED INTO A HUGE MESS?

It is not rare (dare I say "it is common"?) for a newly-hired manager to learn – only *after* they arrive on the job – that they've been dropped into a terrible situation. Didn't they mention the mess during your interview loop? *"No"*. Or during contract negotiations? *"No"*.

Perhaps the Hiring Manager had a good reason for not giving you a head's-up... or maybe not. In either case, your new boss will, of course, want you to clean up the mess left behind. After all, that's why they hired you. Perhaps their secret agenda in evaluating candidates for the job you now have included whether they thought a candidate could handle the logistics and pressures of a post-hurricane repair job.

Fun, fun, fun. However, it does present you with a unique opportunity to emerge as a *turnaround specialist* (as opposed to being viewed as someone who merely keeps the trains running on time). To ensure that you don't get buried by the mess you've been dropped into, you need to be really good at triaging.

CHAPTER 15

TRIAGING URGENT PROBLEMS

If you've been thrown into a mess – read: *emergency* situation – and if it's clearly impossible to fix all the Priority 1 items immediately, then you will need to conduct a *triage exercise* ASAP. Triage is all about making decisions about what most needs to be done first.

Here's how to start your triage process:

1. List all things that need fixing.
2. Place them in *priority order.* (Discuss your prioritization with your manager to ensure that the two of you are on the same page. You might learn some surprising things when you do this – such as what is actually top-of-mind for your manager and skip-level manager.)
3. Determine what needs to be done to fix each problem.
4. Estimate the *required resources* needed to fix each problem.
5. Estimate *how long it will take* to fix each problem, assuming adequate resources. *(See "Chapter 16: Taking Control of the Triage Process" for a method for doing this.)*

Once you've done this, you have some decisions to make:

6. Look for a quick 'win' or two (i.e., low-hanging fruit that can be accomplished in the short term) to gain *momentum*, generate *credibility* for your leadership, and boost *morale.*

    Often, the top-priority items do not lend themselves to quick fixes: but you do not want to go months without achieving some demonstrable success.

Also, you might not have the required resources and time to tackle, say, three high-priority problems, each of which is a big project. So mix it up: figure out how to achieve some short-term successes while your team works on the longer-term successes, which will require a lot of heavy lifting.

Tip: These quick 'wins' do *not* have to be the highest-priority items. You need to prove to your team, to your peers, and your management chain-of-command that change/improvement can happen and is happening – and you need to do that as soon as possible. That will make it a lot easier to get people to "buy into" the near-term and long-terms plans that you develop and that might require additional resources.

7. Pick one of the two top priorities to go after... and develop a plan of action. (Be sure to get your manager's sign-off on your plan of action before you proceed.)
8. Pick a second top priority to go after... and develop a plan of action.

Warning: If you try to knock off only long-term projects, your team and your manager and your manager's manager will not sense progress. I have seen very smart and very capable managers fired or demoted because they were so focused on solving one or two highly complex problems that were such long-term projects that they lost track of the *psychology of the situation.*

Best Practice: Have a mix of projects of varying degrees of difficulty/complexity, so something is accomplished on a regular basis... and the momentum continues, and morale is sustained or improved – with the result that your team and your leadership skills will receive high marks from higher-ups.

CHAPTER 16

TAKING CONTROL OF THE TRIAGE PROCESS

You can't solve all problems at once. You need a method for deciding how to proceed – what to fix first. A "Triage Table" like this one will help you to sort out the messes you are being asked to fix:

Triage Table (*aka* facing reality)					
Problem/ Issue	Priority 1, 2, or 3	How to Fix	Resources Required (e.g., staff, vendors, equipment,)	Budget Needed	Days to Finish

Take a first cut (a rough draft) at filling out this table – and discuss it at a team meeting to get everyone's input. At the team meeting, you might also obtain some context and back-story from team veterans (if they preceded your arrival on the team) about the mess you find yourself in… in which case, you will learn a lot about how things have been run in the past. Guaranteed to be enlightening… and useful.

Incorporate your team's feedback… and then run it by your manager – and then update the Triage Table as necessary. As you keep working through the triage process to develop a *realistic* triage schedule, you might need to tweak the entries in this table. *(See Chapter 17, "Developing a Realistic Triage Schedule".)*

Note: The Triage Table is shorthand for detailed plans or functional specifications, which is required before implementation of a plan can begin.

Here is what you need to provide in the Triage Table (above):

- The "How to Fix?" column needs to consider the following – Processes, Skill-Sets, Strategy, and/or Tactics.
- The "Resources Needed" column needs to include the names of people on your team, people who are not on your team but who are collaborating on the project, vendors (if needed), equipment, office space, and so forth.

As you move through the triaging process, consider the following:

1. Take a long, hard look at the number of Priority 1 items. Can your team tackle more than one Priority 1 item at a time and still keep the trains running? (Your answer depends, of course, on the complexity and scale of the Pri 1 items – and on the resources available to you.)

   Remember: *If everything is a priority, then nothing is a priority.* You need to think strategically about how to proceed because usually it is not possible to fix everything simultaneously.

2. Take a look at the people you listed. If, for example, the names Lola or Beckett appear in the "Resources Required" column too many times on different line items, be aware that the "Days to Finish" must be increased because they can't be working on each of the items full time – and you need to think about moving some of their workload to others so that the stated "Days to Finish" is realistic.

   Warning: *Each project must have discrete resources* – or the estimated "Days to Finish" will be fictional.

3. Stagger your Priority 1 problems (to avoid project collisions as well as insufficient resources and budget) to ensure you succeed in getting multiple problems fixed correctly and on time.
    - Select a long-term (complex) Pri 1 problem to fix. (If you select more than two long-term Pri 1 problems to fix, you're very likely to end up resource-strapped… and some things are sure to fall through the cracks… and you won't be able to show any successes for a long time and/or you'll bust the budget and/or not meet deadlines.)
    - Select a medium-term Pri 1 problem to fix.
    - Select a short-term (low-hanging fruit) Pri 1 problem to fix.
4. Develop a schedule for each issue on the list. (Using a project-scheduling app is a good idea… because it makes it easier to show other managers – your manager, your skip-level manager, and your peers – what's going on and what they can realistically expect.)

Tip: Under-promise and over-deliver.

CHAPTER 17

DEVELOPING A *REALISTIC* TRIAGE SCHEDULE

The common practice is to develop a Work *Forward* schedule. This exercise is *notoriously optimistic* because it squeezes in the last few stages of a project into the remaining amount of time on the schedule, regardless of how much time the work will actually require. This will get you and your team into serious trouble.

"So, what can I do to avoid getting into schedule trouble?" Be sure to develop a Work *Backward* schedule – doing estimates for each stage of the project, beginning with the last stage and working backwards – which will yield a much more realistic schedule.

Here is a time-tested and workplace-hardened optimal process (which I've followed many times) for creating realistic schedules:

1. Develop a **Work *Forward*** schedule for each project, assigning time and resources to the first stage of the project… and progressing to the last stage of the project.

2. Develop a **Work *Backward*** schedule for each project. This involves assigning time and resources to the last stage first, and then to the second-to-last stage, and so on – continuing until you have worked back to the first stage. This process almost always results in more realistic time estimates – *and also results in a longer timeline*, which tells you that the project as defined should have been started weeks or months before your actual start-date. (Yes, an interesting logistics problem.)

3. Focus on the **"Reality Differential"**. Take note of the time/schedule differentials between the Work Forward schedule and the Work Backward schedule – because this will give you a very powerful clue (*aka* "reality differential") about the degree to which your Work Forward schedule is unrealistic.

   ○ If, for example, the Work Forward estimate for project completion is 55 days, and if the Work Backward estimate for project completion is 70 days (and I have many times seen such "discrepancies"), and if your deadline is in 55 days, then there is a 15-day "reality differential"… and loud alarm bells should be going off in your head. (A rapidly beating heart is also a strong clue about reality differentials.)

   ○ If the deadline cannot be moved out – say, it's a hard stop for one business reason or another – then you have some serious thinking to do… and you will then have to have a serious discussion with your manager ASAP.

4. Consider these important variables before meeting with your manager to optimize you chances of pulling off the project by the drop-dead date:

   ○ Cut scope? *(What are your trade-off suggestions?)*

   ○ Redefine the problem/issue? *(What are your thoughts on how to reimagine the project?)*

   ○ Delete one or more features from the list in order to free up resources to tackle the other problems? *(E.g., which features do you think are less important or that you think could be finished not too long after product launch?)*

   ○ Increase full-time staff. *(This is your manager's prerogative, so do* not *suggest.)*

   ○ Increase budget to pull in vendors. *(This is your manager's prerogative, so do* not *suggest.)*

   ○ Push out the schedule – i.e., increase the time allowed to complete a given project? *(This is your manager's prerogative, so do* not *suggest.)*

You might be wondering about the reasoning underlying the phrase *"so do* not *suggest"*. It is a loud alarm bell signaling to you that:

- Your manager is not stupid.
- You need to leave your manager some escape routes and wiggle room so that s-he doesn't feel embarrassed about how powerless s-he is to grant budget and/or resources (which sometimes is transformed into upset with you).
- Your manager might know that s-he cannot grab more resources or budget.
- Your manager might know of coming budget cuts, but can't hint to you about that.
- You don't mention things that you are not in control of (e.g., "asks" for additional budget and warm bodies). Your job, your sphere of influence, is to define the problem – viz., schedule realities – so that your manager understands the situation, which is: the current functional specifications cannot be implemented on schedule as planned *unless* the project is granted more resources and/or more budget and/or a schedule delay.

Your manager will likely initiate a resources-and-budget-and-deadline discussion with your skip-level manager. That said, it's possible that your manager will immediately say to you, "What do you need to pull this off within the current schedule?"

Best Practice: You should be *fully prepared* to answer that question *on the spot* (because you have brilliantly anticipated this possibility and have done your homework). Having that answer at-the-ready provides your manager with the details s-he needs to make decisions about schedule, budget, and people resources as well as to present the sober realities to your skip-level manager, if necessary.

Now it's time to have a heart-to-heart talk with your manager. Come prepared with:

- *Suggested trade-offs* that can be made to shorten the schedule of some of the items in the overall project (incorporating input from your

Direct Reports), but not mentioning budget or resources needed. For example:

- ○ Cut scope?
- ○ Simplify or eliminate services or features?
- ○ Eliminate some spec-review meetings and bypass some second-level stakeholders? (Dangerous, but if you're desperate...)
- ○ Put aside late-in-arriving Design Change Requests until version 2.0 of the service or product?
- ○ Push out the schedule?

- *Project Schedule print-outs.*
  - ○ Bring a print-out of your recommended approaches, *but also* bring print-outs for your second and third recommendations. Managers respond very favorably when their Direct Report managers present them with options, for two reasons:
    - ▪ It demonstrates that you have thought deeply and carefully about the issues (which you have, of course, done).
    - ▪ It provides your manager with some wiggle room (which is also wiggle room for you... in case your manager doesn't like your recommended approach).

    Warning: Managers, like most people, do not like ultimatums. No one likes being backed into a corner.

Tip: Managers too often "delegate" a long list of problems that need fixing, without being clear about the priorities of the problems on the list and/or without knowing what it will take to do each fix... so it's important that you provide a reality-check to your manager.

Sometimes managers are antsy because the problems have been around for a while and were not solved by the previous manager, so your manager is counting on you to be a miracle worker.

Warning: If your manager was promoted just before you arrived, the "previous manager" who didn't solve the problems might be the very manager you now have… so tread cautiously and avoid criticism about what was done or not done before you arrived on the scene.

Your manager might be under strong pressure from your skip-level manager's unrealistic expectations… and might not feel at liberty to discuss that with you. So if your manager makes a decision that doesn't make the most sense to you, there's a good chance that there are "hidden factors" that your manager has to live with – and that, consequently, you have to live with.

Remember: This meeting provides a great opportunity to flush out your manager's thoughts and actual priorities.

- ○ This discussion might give you important clues, which might provide you with an indirect peek into upper management's priorities and thinking.
  - ▪ This is an opportunity to observe your manager's temperament and how s-he approaches triaging and making trade-offs.

Warning: Your manager will usually try to pressure you to do more with insufficient time, budget, and resources (perhaps because they, too, are under pressure). They will challenge you or threaten you with phrases like "We need you to step up" or "This is a great opportunity for you to prove yourself" or "If you don't get this done on time, on budget, and meet the quality bar, both of us will be looking for jobs" or "We hired you because we thought you could get the job done".

Do not be intimidated. The more prepared you are, the more comfortable you will be in resisting such pressure – and the more skilled you will be at educating your manager by presenting the realities *and* offering options (and a risk-benefit analysis).

Note for recently-hired managers: You might be asking yourself, *"Why won't management cough up additional resources or budget if they want these Priority 1's done ASAP?"* Well, if you're asking that, welcome to corporate realities.

Experienced managers do not give an unproven manager more resources until the manager has demonstrated an ability to make efficient use of existing resources. If you deliver one or two projects on time and on budget as well as meet or exceed the quality bar, then your credibility goes up, way up – and your manager, who now has more confidence in your leadership and operational skills, is then much more likely to find additional resources for you (unless constrained by your skip-level manager).

But don't expect that to happen in the first month or two or three. You're being watched and evaluated to determine whether you're a good credit risk. If you're a relative unknown (*aka* newcomer), you'll have to deliver some 'wins' so that upper management is convinced that giving you and your team more resources and budget is a wise business investment.

PART FIVE

HIRING GREAT PEOPLE –
THE FIRST STEP

CHAPTER 18

HIRING IS THE MOST IMPORTANT THING YOU DO

If you think that hiring is a *tactical* task rather than a *strategic* task, then repeat after me:

> *"Hiring is the most important specific task I do as a manager.*
> *Hiring is the most important specific task I do as a manager.*
> *Hiring is the most important specific task I do as a manager."*

Here are some of the reasons that hiring is indeed your most important discrete activity:

- Hiring has long-lasting effects on your team's productivity, on your other Direct Reports, on you, and on the company. If a mistake is made, you will pay for that mistake for a long time.
- Hiring is a costly and time-consuming process, involving numerous people and departments, so you want to accomplish this task in the most efficient manner possible.
- Once you have hired someone, the company invests in orientation, classroom training, training on the job, and supervision, which are also expensive and time-consuming.
- A Great Hire increases the chance that your team's quality bar will be raised and productivity will be increased. A Bad Hire has the opposite effect. (A Good Hire keeps the trains running… but doesn't raise the quality bar.)

- The new hire will affect team morale. You want to hire someone who will improve team morale if it needs improving – and not undermine it if team morale is already high.
- If the new hire doesn't work out, your "credit rating" will go down. Your Direct Reports, your manager, your skip-level manager, and H.R. will be wondering, *"What went wrong?"* and *"Why did that person get hired?"* (Guess whom they'll point their fingers at? Yup, rightly or wrongly, the blame will be heading in your direction at lightning speed.)
- It can be very difficult to get rid of a new hire without jumping through lots of hoops (H.R., Legal, et cetera).
- Getting rid of a Bad Hire will have a number of effects on your Direct Reports, whether they like or dislike the new person.

So keep in mind that *optimal hiring is a strategic goal.* Ergo, it's very important to have an optimal methodology for the interview-loop process.

"How do I ensure that the people I hire will be Great Hires?" Read on…

CHAPTER 19

GREAT HIRING BEGINS WITH
TOP-OF-THE-LINE JOB DESCRIPTIONS

I'm assuming that you will write an accurate and detailed Job Description, that H.R. will post that J.D. and screen dozens of candidates within the context of that J.D., and that H.R. will then pass the 5-10 most-promising Resumes to you. I am also assuming that you will make the final decision about which 3-5 candidates have backgrounds that are best aligned with the J.D. and with your team's needs going forward – and you will ask H.R. to bring in the candidates you've selected for an interview loop.

Warning: Do *not* simply recycle a previous Job Description – despite the temptation to do so when you're harried and short on time. The road to Hell is paved with out-of-date and non-compelling J.D.s. The responsibilities of jobs morph over time and strategies morph over time – and require different skillsets and experience.

If you want to attract potential Great Hires, you need to own the J.D. and make it a Priority 1 to ensure that it's a world-class J.D. You might be missing out on great candidates because the J.D. that they read is not accurate – so they don't apply for the open position.

I have many times heard managers say that they didn't have the time to write a new J.D. Why did they say that? Because crafting a top-notch Job Description was not a high-enough priority in their minds. The result was often a non-aligned winnowing process by H.R., followed by a more-difficult-than-is-necessary winnowing by the Hiring Manager, followed by less-than-optimal interview loops. The result was a less-than-optimal new hire – or a no-hire. If the result was a Bad Hire, then a lot of time, money, and effort will have been wasted – and if no one was hired, the process has to be started all over again.

A top-notch J.D. is the very important first step in hiring Great People. Don't take shortcuts. Create a detailed, accurate, up-to-date, nuanced, and professional-looking Job Description... and make it compelling. Run it by H.R. for feedback and sign-off. (And if you're a relatively new manager, be sure to run the J.D. by your manager.)

> **Best practice:** Have your Direct Reports vet the J.D. *(but see "Warning", below)*. This vetting improves team morale: it is, after all, *their* future teammate. Your Directs will often catch errors in the J.D. and also make suggestions on how to improve the J.D.

> **Warning:** Get your Directs' input only if you are certain that there will not be any unintended consequences – jealousies, frustrations, or feelings of being underappreciated. In certain circumstances vetting by Directs could be the *wrong thing* to do. For example, your Directs should not vet the J.D. if:
>
> - Your team doesn't know yet that a new position is being created.
> - Sharing the J.D. might tip off the team (and others via word-of-mouth) to an as-yet-unannounced re-org.
> - Sharing the J.D. might make some team members wonder why you didn't "promote" them (without an interview loop) into the position.
> - Sharing the J.D. might encourage your Direct Reports to suggest alterations to the J.D. that would benefit them... because they plan to apply for the job.

CHAPTER 20

CRAFTING A TOP-OF-THE-LINE JOB DESCRIPTION

As I've already mentioned, too many managers recycle an old Job Description. Jobs evolve, circumstances change. What previously was an acceptable J.D. for the position in question might no longer be up-to-snuff.

> **Remember:** *Hiring is the most important thing you do*, the thing that has the longest-term consequences – for you, for your team, and for your company.

Here are some of the reasons why creating a world-class J.D. should be a top priority:

- A top-notch J.D. will increase the odds of attracting the best candidates.
- A top-notch J.D. will save you embarrassment in interviews when you have to explain to the candidates what is missing from the J.D. and what is no longer relevant on the J.D.
- You will lose credibility with your team because they will wonder why you posted a misleading or out-of-date or sub-par J.D.
- You might lose credibility with H.R. and your manager if they learn that the J.D. that you provided was not accurate or up-to-date.
- You might lose top candidates when, late in the process, they hear about the additional or different or no-longer-relevant job

requirements. They might even feel that either there's a little bit of bait-and-switch going on or that the organization doesn't have its act together, either of which would send a negative message about you, your team, and your company.

The following J.D. template will help you get off to a good start in crafting a top-of-the-line Job Description.

Job Title *<J.D. template>*

Position Description – Provide a general description of what the job entails and what the person is expected to accomplish. Make clear whether the position is primarily that of a sole contributor... or that of being part of a collaborative team... or that of being a supervisor or manager.

Requirements of the Position – Describe the general responsibilities as well as the specific day-to-day tasks (in a bulleted list) and longer-term tasks (in a bulleted list) that are mandatory and critical to success.

Key Competencies – Provide specifics (in a bulleted list) of the skills and abilities that the position requires. Include technical skills, soft skills.

Key Experiences – Provide specifics (in a bulleted list) of the relevant experiences required, the number of years of experience required, and whether vertical-industry knowledge is required.

Education

Certifications & Continuing Education

Additional preferred Knowledge, Skills, and/or Training – Provide specifics (in a bulleted list)

Languages – If a language in addition to your country's native language is required, specify the level of proficiency required: e.g., basic conversational, sophisticated conversational, reading ability, writing ability, and translation ability (written and/or oral). If a specialized vocabulary is needed, note that.

PART SIX

HIRING GREAT PEOPLE –
THE INTERVIEW LOOP

CHAPTER 21

AN INTERVIEW IS NOT A CONVERSATION

(Did You Think It Was?)

A n interview is an *information-gathering exercise.* You (and your team) need to be clear – very clear – about what information you are most interested in collecting… and then collect it in an efficient manner. You need to plan, prepare, and coordinate.

> **Caution:** Some candidates are very skilled at being friendly and getting an interviewer into a general conversation that simulates an informal conversation between friends. At this point, you are not their friend, and they are not your friend – but if they have sucked you into "friendship mode", they are controlling the interview.

> **Remember:** You need *information* that allows you to make a critical hiring decision – and you need to get that information from them within a limited amount of time. You need to be extremely efficient at doing that – as do the other people who are interviewing the candidates. You don't have to be unfriendly or heavy-handed: act professionally – courteous, welcoming, straightforward – but don't for a second lose track of the fact that you're doing the interview to *gather information.*

CHAPTER *22*

STRATEGIC PLANNING FOR AN INTERVIEW LOOP

" *You think that hiring someone requires a strategy?"* Yes… because hiring *is* a strategic activity – one that has crucial long-term consequences.

Strategy is all about winning – so you need to hire Great People to build a Great Team that can beat the competition. Therefore, a *world-class hiring procedure* is a key strategy – and that procedure requires a carefully thought-out process that you and your team needs to master.

You and the other interviewers you select to participate in the interview loop *must be on the same page* about the Vision and Mission for your team, your unit, your company – and must be 100% clear about *what your team most needs in its next hire.* When smart and experienced candidates hear different versions of company and team realities, they understandably get nervous about what they might be getting themselves into if they accept a job on your team.

Remember: Smart candidates, sophisticated candidates, will ask different interviewers the same question in order to find out whether there is a single reality or multiple realities or hidden agendas.

Chapter 23

Whom Will You Choose to Interview the Candidates?

E ach of your Direct Reports should interview candidates from outside your company.

Best Practice: At least one of these interviews should be a joint interview – i.e., two members of your team conduct a joint interview with the candidate. *(For an explanation of why joint interviews are an important safety net, see Chapter 36: "The 'Chameleon Candidate' Nightmare".)*

If you have, say, more than six Direct Reports, joint interviews can serve multiple purposes. Joint interviews give more team members an opportunity to participate. They also help your Directs to hone their interviewing skills – especially those who haven't had much interviewing experience, which is very important because everyone needs good interviewing skills.

Pair up an experienced interviewer (the role model) with someone who has less experience in interviewing candidates, which provides in-service training in a peer-counseling set-up.

If there is a team with whom you collaborate closely, and if the person you will be hiring will be working closely with that team, think about trying to get the peer manager of that team to interview the candidates. If there are 3-5 candidates, this is a serious time commitment to request of a peer manager – and they might not be able to free up time to interview all the candidates. Here are some options:

- If you have more than one peer manager with whom you work closely, perhaps you can get each of them to interview at least one or two candidates if they don't have time to interview all 3-5 candidates.
- Involve peer managers only after you have narrowed the field to two finalists.
- Allow the peer managers to select one of their Direct Reports with good interviewing skills to act as a proxy.

Caution: If the working relationship with your peer manager's team is especially close, you could invite the peer manager to do joint interviews with you (perhaps only with the two finalists). This is an unusual approach that should be used both sparingly and cautiously, because it has two significant downsides:

- ○ The candidates won't have as much direct time with you, and they want to get a good "read" on their potential future manager.
- ○ You won't have as much time to do your usual follow-up questioning in order to get to know the candidate as thoroughly as you want to before making a hiring decision.

Tip: You can add 15-20 minutes at the end of your joint interview so that you have some 1-on-1 time with the candidate.

Your manager might want to interview the candidates, especially if you are hiring a manager who will report to you. If your manager is on a tight schedule, perhaps s-he would be satisfied interviewing only the top one or two candidates. (If your manager has reason to trust your hiring acumen, they will welcome the opportunity to say, "I pass. It's your job to do.")

Best Practice: You, the Hiring Manager, should always *go last* on each interview loop so that you see all the feedback of the earlier interviewers and can follow up on any loose ends or issues that have been raised.

Best Practice: Provide your Direct Reports and any other interviewers with the Resumes of all candidates *at least 2 days before* the day of the interview loop so that each interviewer has sufficient time to study the Resumes.

Too often interviewers get copies of the Resumes the morning of the interview loop… which means that they will not have time to study the Resumes before interviewing the candidates. As a result, the interviewer does a quick-study of the Resume *during the interview* – repeatedly losing eye contact with the candidate – while the candidate sits there, bored and unimpressed by interviewers. Such behavior by interviewers is not a good advertisement for the professionalism of your team or of the company.

Remember: Bad word-of-mouth travels fast on the grapevine – both inside a company and within an industry – and can seriously undermine future attempts to recruit Great Hires to your team. You do not want external candidates bad-mouthing your team to their friends or to others in your industry… and you do not want internal candidates to bad-mouth your team to others inside the company.

Your job, as the Hiring Manager, is make it clear to interviewers that you select that you expect them to courteous, respectful, focused, and businesslike with every candidate.

CHAPTER 24

THORNY ISSUE – HOW TO DEAL WITH INTERNAL CANDIDATES

What if someone on your team applies for the position? Or someone from another team who is well-known to some of your Direct Reports? Some of the factors that you need to consider are:

- Internal candidates might prefer to keep confidential the fact they are interviewing. (They might fear humiliation if teammates or others known to them learn that they interviewed for the job – and didn't get the job.)
- You, the Hiring Manager, might prefer to keep this fact confidential.
- You cannot have your Direct Reports interviewing one of their peers or a friend from another team... so you will need to find neutral interviewers.

"How should I handle the internal-candidate situation?" Here is what you need to keep top-of-mind, regardless of whether the candidate is one of your Directs or an internal candidate from another unit or another division:

- If you have worked with the Direct Report candidate for a substantial amount of time, you might know all you need to know about the candidate. If not, begin by intelligence gathering on your Direct Report.
  - If you are a new manager with your current team (say, in your first month on the job), you will need to:

- Study past performance reviews.
    - Meet with your peer managers to see whether they can provide feedback.
    - Chat with the previous manager(s) of your internal candidate.
  - The same intelligence-gathering drill applies if the internal candidate is from *another team* in your company... but *only if* you are sure that the candidate has openly requested permission to interview from her/his manager.
    - The candidate might be interviewing *without* their manager's permission or knowledge, in which case you must respect their privacy (if H.R. policy allows such confidentiality). Yes, this will make gathering intelligence about the candidate more difficult.
    - If the candidate requests confidentiality, H.R. might be able to help by providing some information.
    - Be sure to discuss the candidate's desire for confidentiality with your manager, who might know a good deal about the candidate.
    - Consider having your manager interview internal candidates because that can help to ensure confidentiality. Also, they can serve as a more objective judge if you feel too close to the internal candidate

Nota Bene: It's very important to give internal candidates (especially those from your team) a shot at a job opening... even if you have already determined that they are not likely to be the top candidate for the position.

"Why is it critical that your Direct Report candidates feel that they have been given a fair shake, given a real opportunity to advance within their current unit?" Because if they feel that no door is open to them, they will leave – physically or emotionally – neither of which you want. Also, it's terrible for your entire team's morale to deny one of them an opportunity without a fair hearing.

Have a pre-interview with your Direct Report candidates – before determining whether to put them through an interview loop. This can be a valuable learning experience. You get to know them better; you learn why they want this position rather than the one they already hold; you learn what they might bring to the table that they are not currently bringing to the table. And you have a chance to do some career coaching to help them identify what they can do to become a stronger candidate for future opportunities.

Best Practice: If you do decide to put an internal candidate through an interview loop, select some peer managers – preferably managers of teams that collaborate with your team – to be interviewers. You cannot have other of your Direct Reports interview a teammate or an internal candidate known to them. Similarly, you can't use a peer manager who manages or has managed the internal candidate to interview the candidate. (You can talk privately to such a peer manager if such a situation arises.)

Bringing in seasoned managers or veteran sole contributors from other teams will lend an aura of objectivity: if the internal candidate does not get the job, you can let that candidate know what the feedback was (without naming names of who said what), which can be very valuable information for the internal candidate.

CHAPTER 25

THE HIRING MANAGER'S LASER FOCUS ON MOTIVATION, TEAM FIT, AND UPSIDE POTENTIAL

L et's assume that the candidate has been vetted by H.R. and by you for appropriateness of background and skillset. This vetting process usually includes H.R. doing background checks and speaking with select candidates on the telephone to get some clarifications of the positions, skills, and experiences listed on the candidates' resumes. (The Hiring Manager also has the option of doing a phone screen of, say, 5-8 candidates in order to winnow the list down to 3-5 candidates for H.R. to invite in for an interview loops.)

Let's further assume that during the interview loop you will have other interviewers determine whether the candidate has the necessary experience, relevant skills, domain-knowledge, and/or technical chops. So what's different about your role on this interview loop?

As the Hiring Manager, it is critical that you focus on three things:

- What motivates the candidate (other than "money" or "promotion" or "need a change" or "prestige")?
- Will the candidate be a good team fit?
- Does the candidate have substantial upside potential?

Of course, all interviewers should think about these three things – but they won't all have the necessary experience or skill to do that well.

So it's critical that you get a good "read" on motivation, team fit, and upside potential.

CHAPTER 26

WHO ASKS WHICH QUESTIONS?

Schedule a pre-interview-loop prep meeting with your Direct Reports (and other interviewers you select) to decide who will cover what topics and who will ask which questions.

Do I hear you groaning? Perhaps you think that this is overkill. Stop groaning... and take a deep breath – and let me give you one of many examples of why this is important.

I remember an occasion in which I was the Hiring Manager and the last interviewer on the loop. Halfway through the interview, I asked the candidate to discuss her strengths and weaknesses... and she replied: *"That's the fifth time I've been asked that question today."* That was an embarrassing situation – and the candidate was not impressed. It made me and my team look unprofessional – uncoordinated, unprepared, disorganized, inconsiderate – which could make a top-notch, savvy candidate think, *"Do I really want to join a team and an organization that doesn't have its act together?"*

Even the people who you do *not* hire should go away with a lasting impression of you and your team as a group of first-class professionals – and they will spread the word. Over time other top-notch candidates will be eager to join your team and your company.

Also, having a number of interviewers go over the same ground is a colossal waste of time. That time could be better used to ask additional questions or to dig deeper with follow-up questions so that you end up with a Great Hire.

Remember: No one interviewer can ask all the key questions. That's why it's important for you to assign areas of responsibility to and specific questions for each interviewer – ahead of time

Tip: It's a good idea (and a courtesy) to include those peer managers participating in the interview loop in this exercise; however, it's often very difficult to make that happen because it probably is not a Pri 1 meeting for them. So you can either let such managers conduct their interview the way they are accustomed to doing – or you can suggest some topics and questions in an email.

CHAPTER 27

THE QUESTION-AND-ANSWER GAME

You can find tons of sample interview questions on the Internet. You can also find *recommended answers* on the Internet – and you can bet that conscientious, aggressive, experienced, intelligent, and thoughtful candidates will do their homework and be amply prepared to do a good job of answering predictable questions.

But are such well-prepared candidates the best candidates, the ones who might be Great Hires? Well, yes... and no. Such candidates are clearly smart, ambitious, tactical, detail-oriented, and competitive. Such traits can serve your team and your company well.

That said, there are other, equally valuable (and perhaps more valuable) traits such as interpersonal skills, collaboration skills, out-of-the-box thinking, strategic thinking, big-picture vision, mediation skills, team-player attitude, writing skills, and analytic thinking. These traits are more difficult to ferret out – but *that* is the goal of an interview loop. The candidate you hire must bring the right stuff to the table and be a good team fit. If a candidate is not a good team fit, then you don't hire that person – because team productivity and morale would be hurt.

"So, what are the most important questions to ask candidates?" The answer is: *follow-up questions.*

Your initial questions are *warm-up questions.* The candidates' initial (rehearsed) answers are often predictable. You certainly won't learn much that is useful if candidates merely rehash their Resumes or their rehearsed career narratives. Rather, you want to learn how the candidates think, how they respond to difficult challenges, whether they bounce back from mistakes and failures, and what they've learned from their mistakes or from difficult experiences.

"How do I learn that?"

You learn that by asking *follow-up questions.* But you can't ask a follow-up question unless you first ask a warm-up question. The next two chapters address warm-up questions and follow-up questions.

CHAPTER *28*

WARM-UP QUESTIONS

No one person can ask all the warm-up questions in this chapter – so a subset of these questions should be distributed among the interviewers on the loop.

Depending on the type of position that you are hiring for – e.g., sole contributor, supervisor, manager – some of the following questions will be more relevant than others. So cull the list and make use of the questions that are most appropriate to the position that you are trying to fill… and, of course, add your own questions.

- "What is the toughest situation you've ever been in professionally?"

  (can reveal a candidate's descriptive skills, degree of forthrightness, and how the candidate thinks and acts – i.e., makes choices – in difficult circumstances; also reveals whether the candidate has ever survived a trial by fire and/or whether a candidate is able or willing to discuss, frankly, what was an uncomfortable and perhaps unflattering chapter in her/his work-life)

- "What do you want to be doing in 5 years? in 10 years?"

  (can reveal whether candidate has a career plan, thinks ahead; sometimes reveals that the open position that the candidate is applying for bears no relationship to the hoped-for career trajectory; you might also sense a reluctance to discuss this topic because the candidate does not want to telegraph long-range plans and ambitions; and if the candidate has been in the work force 5 years or more and says

something along the lines of "I don't know", the chances are high that they are either being disingenuous — as in, intentionally not revealing what they really want to do — or that they perhaps are not smart enough or thoughtful enough to be on your team)

- "Why should this company spend time, money, and effort to get you up-to-speed? What's unique about you?" <for external candidates only>

  (can reveal the candidate's self-image, what value-add the candidate brings to the position and team, and whether the candidate has a tendency to over-sell or under-sell themselves; also, can reveal whether the candidate does big-picture thinking about how a company thinks about its employees)

- "Why would the people on my team want to work with you?"

  (can reveal whether and how the candidate self-assesses and also gives clues about the candidate's degree of situational self-awareness and psychological sophistication)

- "Do you want to become a manager in this company? (If the candidate says "yes", then ask, "Why would people here want to work for you?")

  (can reveal whether the candidate — if not applying for a managerial role — has managerial aspirations; can also reveal whether the candidate has thought about which personal attributes and characteristics would make her/him appealing to Direct Reports and to upper management)

- "What did you do in the past 5 years that you are most proud of?"

  (can reveal not only what the candidate is proud of but also, more importantly, why the candidate is proud of that; also can reveal whether the candidate is most proud of something they have done recently, say, within the last 12 months)

- "What side projects have you worked on in the past 2 years?"

  (can reveal whether the candidate has been given or has asked for "stretch" projects — beyond the core work-load — or has been motivated to devise a self-initiated skunk-works project)

- "Tell me your two best customer stories – either an internal customer or an external customer?"

  (can reveal the candidate's degree of sophistication re a customer-service mentality; can also give clues about what the candidate is most proud of, and perhaps clues about how the candidate goes about succeeding; if the candidate has not had external customers, ask about internal customers – i.e., people inside the company who rely on the candidate's performance)

- "What is the most unpleasant situation in the workplace that you have had to deal with?"

  (can reveal how the candidate confronts a problem and develops a strategy or set of tactics to address the situation; also can provide clues about what types of conditions push the candidate's buttons)

- "What were the two worst mistakes you've made in your career?"

  (can reveal whether the candidate is comfortable talking about failure in an adult manner – and leads to finding out whether the candidate learns from mistakes; if the candidate can't think of anything, or pauses a long, long time, that's at least an orange flag and perhaps a red flag about openness and integrity – though it's always possible that the candidate has not made any big mistakes yet.

  Note: If the open position is entry level or lower level and the candidate has been in the workforce for only a few years, make it "the worst single mistake" – and if the candidate has only had only one job for 1 year, skip this question.

- "Which of your previous jobs forced you to work the hardest?"

  (can reveal whether a candidate has ever worked really hard and what made that particular job the one in which s-he had to work the hardest; also gives a clue about what "hardest" means to the candidate – long hours? difficult task technically? intra-team or cross-team collaboration issues? opinions about the manager?)

- "What work-related books have you read in the past year?" *and* "What work-related magazines and newspapers do you read regularly?" *and* "Are there work-related websites or blogs that you follow?"

  (can reveal the degree to which "self-improvement" and "continual education" is a part of the candidate's mind-set)

- "What continuing-education courses have you taken and what conferences have you attended in the past 3 years?"

  (can reveal the degree to which "self-improvement" and "continual education" is a part of the candidate's mind-set)

  Note: Take into consideration whether the candidate's previous/ current employer pays for or subsidizes continuing education and conference fees; if the candidate has not been given the opportunity to take a continuing-education course or attend a conference, ask only about self-improvement self-study – e.g., which books or magazines? which newspapers? which free online courses? which free lectures?

- "Describe for me, without mentioning the name of the person or the name of the company, who your favorite manager was? Why was that person your favorite?" <followed by> "Describe the least favorite manager you've had? Again, don't mention the name of the person or the company."

  (can reveal what the candidate wants or needs from a manager – and allows you to think about whether you're the right manager for this candidate; also, if the candidate slips up and gives the name of the person or the company, that can be a clue about attention to detail, listening skills, and an ability to mentally multi-task.)

- "What are you really good at?"

  (a softer way of asking about "strengths"... and tells you how the candidate self-assesses... or perhaps what they think they should be saying because they studied the J.D. carefully and want their "strengths" to align with the J.D.)

- "What are you less good at?"

  (a nicer way of asking about "weaknesses"… and tends to more easily get a candidate to address "weaknesses"; also, this question and the previous question will tell you a lot about how comfortable the candidate is in being straightforward.)

CHAPTER 29

FOLLOW-UP QUESTIONS
(*AKA* PENETRATING THE FAÇADE)

Follow-up questions are the way you break through the rehearsed responses to fairly standard interview questions and discover more useful information about the candidate's character, thinking processes, and actual experience. (Some of the warm-up questions in the previous chapter sometimes get you past rehearsed answers, but more often they are what allow you to ask the follow-up questions.)

Here are some examples of follow-up questions that allow you to drill down and find out more about the candidate. Some of them ask nearly the same question in a slightly different way, but certain ones might follow more smoothly from the candidate's answer to the warm-up question.

- "Why did you decide to do that?" or, "Why did you decide to do it that way?"

    (can reveal how candidate thinks about alternatives and trade-offs)

- "What options did you consider? Why did you eliminate those options?"

    (can reveal how the candidate goes about problem-solving and triaging)

- "How else might you have handled that situation? And what do you think the outcomes would have been from those alternative solutions?"

(can reveal whether the candidate ponders outcomes and considers the consequences of more than just one approach)

- "In retrospect, would you do the same thing?"

  (can reveal whether the candidate thinks about past experiences and whether s-he incorporates learnings from those experiences)

  o If the candidate responds *"Yes"*, ask "Why?"
  o If the candidate responds *"No"*, ask "What would you do differently if you could do it over again?")

- "I'm not clear on your thought process. Could you say that again, but in different words?"

  (can reveal how well a candidate can recast a response)

- "Did your teammates agree with your approach?" (or, if more appropriate: "Did your peers agree with your proposed solution?")

  (can reveal degree to which the candidate collaborates, seeks input, and/or is aware or cares about what others think)

- "Did your manager agree with your proposed solution?"

  (can reveal whether candidate is in synch with management)

- "Was this your chosen direction? Or did your manager or higher-ups dictate how to fix the problem?"

  (can reveal whether the candidate owned the solution or was taking orders)

- "If you were faced with the same situation today, what would you do the same? and what would you do differently?"

  (can reveal whether the candidate learns from experience and/or from managerial mentoring)

- "Why didn't you become a <type of job or career>? You could have chosen that as your career path. From what you've told me and what your Resume shows, that would have been a logical choice."

  (can reveal whether candidate has thought about their long-term

career choices or whether and how they view their own evolution as a professional)

- "If your *current* manager <or *former* manager> were sitting here, which of your answers would that manager agree with and which would s-he not agree with?"

    (can reveal whether the candidate can view themselves through their manager's eyes; also reveals how comfortable they are with discussing the relationship to the manager)

- "Did you make that decision after long deliberation? Or was it a quick call that you made on gut instinct?"

    (can reveal the candidate's style of decision-making)

- "What was the most difficult thing about choosing that solution?"

    (can reveal whether the candidate thought deeply about alternative solutions)

- "In your current role, what do you most enjoy doing?" *(And after the candidate answers…)* "What do you least enjoy doing?" *(And after the candidate answers…)* "What would you change about your current job (other than salary) to make you want to stay in it?"

    (can reveal whether the candidate has thought about how to improve the job or whether they accept the given realities; also provides clues about what the candidate would most like to be doing and what motivates the candidate)

- "Have you ever had to carry out a policy that you disagreed with or that you didn't feel good about? *(And if the candidate answers 'yes'…)* "How did you manage that?" *(And after the candidate answers…)* "What was the outcome of that?" *(And after the candidate answers…)* "Did that experience affect your choice of job or career in the following years?"

    (can reveal integrity and strength of conviction or self-preserving stoicism)

- "How would you improve our company's business?"

    (can reveal whether an external candidate is familiar with your company's business model and its products and/or services)

    Note: Some candidates might be reluctant to answer this question because their ideas have previously been ripped off by companies that did not hire them, so their reluctance is understandable; if so, you will learn how well the candidates explain their reluctance, if any, which gives strong clues about integrity and forthrightness; an internal candidate should have thoughts on this topic)

Remember: Follow-up questions allow you to learn, in greater depth, who candidates really are: how they think, how they react to probing questions, and whether their prepared script – the narrative about themselves that they have crafted and rehearsed – holds up under scrutiny. It also gives you a sense of how rapidly they think on their feet and, perhaps, whether they are out-of-the-box thinkers.

CHAPTER 30

REAL-TIME FEEDBACK IS CRITICAL

It is vital that every interviewer contribute to the real-time email "conversation" about *each candidate* going through an all-day interview loop. *"Why?"* Because real-time feedback has the following benefits:

- When interviewers provide feedback immediately, the details of the interview are fresh in their minds... and they can sometimes quote the candidate's response to a specific question that was especially revealing.
- The previous interviewer might comment that *"I planned to ask the candidate about <xxx>, but I ran out of time. Will someone please ask about that?"* – and the next interview can do that.
- The next interviewer notes the orange and red flags (if any) that have been raised by the previous interviewer – and then can choose to do a deep dive into those areas.
- The "rolling feedback" decreases the chance of "question redundancy", which makes a bad impression on candidates.
- The "rolling feedback" increases knowledge that successive interviewers have about the candidate.

Real-time feedback makes the interview loop far more effective and insightful.

Best Practice: If each interview is slotted for 1 hour, then each interview should end after 50 minutes... so that the interviewer has 5 minutes to provide written feedback – and so that the next interviewer has 5 minutes to read the preceding feedback before the candidate shows up. (In some cases, the interviewer who just finished might even want to walk down the hallway to the next interviewer to relate something in person.) This timing also give candidates some time for a bio-break or a liquid refreshment or snack before the next interview, which is a consideration that candidates really appreciate (and which they remember when they do their postmortem of the interview loop with their friends and advisors).

Best Practice: Interviewers should all be required to write *more-detailed, complete feedback immediately after* they send an email with their brief, real-time feedback. (If that is not possible, more complete feedback should be sent no later than the end of the day.) This longer feedback should include details on the candidate's answers to certain questions. The questions and the candidate's answer should be rendered as close to the actual words as possible. (E.g., *"When I asked the candidate about X, s-he replied: <direct quote or close paraphrase>."*)

The Hiring Manager (that's you!) will learn a lot from "hearing" the actual language of the candidates as they answered various questions throughout the day.

An Efficient Format for Real-Time Feedback

The table, below, shows an effective format for *real-time, brief* email feedback that every interviewer on the loop sends out to everyone on the interview loop *immediately after* completing an interview.

Real-time feedback format *<template>*

Pros	(list up to three strengths that you think the candidate has; no sentences or paragraphs for now – just brief phrases in bullet-list form)
Cons	(list up to three weaknesses that you think the candidate has; no sentences or paragraphs for now – just brief phrases in bullet-list form)
Follow-up recommendations	(if there are topics that you think need more exploration and that you didn't have time for, be specific about what additional questions one of the following interviewers should ask)
Concerns	(in 1-2 sentences, mention any concerns that you might have)
Summary	(2-3 sentences about your impressions of the candidate; later you can write up more detailed and complete comments and send them to every interviewer on the loop by the end of the day)
Hire or No Hire	(Vote "Hire" or "No Hire" – without further explanation: those are the only two options)

Note: A fuller evaluation of each candidate by each interviewer should be written and sent to the Hiring Manager ASAP – and in no case later than by end of day.

"Maybe" or "Perhaps" or "Not Sure" Is Not Allowed

"Why are Hire and No Hire the only two options?" Because you should only hire people about whom you feel very positive, very certain, very excited. And, of course, you can't "maybe hire" someone or be "not sure" about whether you want to hire the candidate.

You either hire them… or you don't.

Some of your Direct Reports, particularly if they are new to being included in interview loops, might want more time to decide. But there isn't more time… as you will be sure to remind them. Your team needs to learn that one does not feel ambivalent when interviewing a candidate judged to be a Great Hire. We usually feel ambivalent only when we are unsure… and "unsure" does not meet the quality bar for a Great Hire.

> **Tip:** When a potentially Great Hire is on your doorstep, you and your Directs will be thinking and should be feeling: *"I want to grab this person before someone else does."*

Making weighty decisions *quickly* is, for many people, an uncomfortable situation and often is an acquired skill – and one of the arenas in which this becomes evident is in the hiring process. Members of your team will learn how to do that – especially those who aspire to be a manager someday – and you are the role model and mentor for teaching others on your team how to make excellent decisions quickly when that is necessary.

CHAPTER 31

DID THE CANDIDATE HAVE ANY QUESTIONS FOR YOU, THE HIRING MANAGER?

A serious external candidate, who is prepared and smart, will have questions about your company's business and culture as well as about your team and how you run it.

Yes, the candidate with no questions might have had their basic questions answered by H.R. during the screening process – e.g., questions about benefits, salary, medical plan, vacation, et cetera. That is not sufficient. Top candidates should have questions, especially for you – the Hiring Manager – that give you a sense of their curiosity, their professional pride, the way they view their career, and their level of engagement. If a candidate doesn't have questions, think twice about hiring that candidate… but also be sure to consider the following caveats:

Caveat: Be sure to allow for cultural differences. In some cultures and in some countries, it is *not* OK to ask a potential boss pointed questions.

Caveat: An internal candidate from elsewhere in the company might already know, through the grapevine (or because they have a friend on your team), most of what they need to know about you and your team and your goals – or they would not have applied for the position.

Also, an internal candidate from your team probably does not need to ask you questions about your team, though they might have questions about the new position if it's different from any role that you have on your team (rather than filling a role that already exists but that someone will be leaving or has already left.)

Best Practice: The candidate might have asked their questions earlier in the loop, perhaps preferring to hear about the "team reality" directly from your Direct Reports rather than from the Hiring Manager. That's perfectly OK.

But if the candidate – external or internal – does not ask you any questions, email everyone on the interview loop and ask: *"Did the candidate ask you any questions about our team, our culture, our goals, and/or our company?"*

Best Practice: If the candidate did not ask you any questions by the end of the interview, always ask, *"Do you have any questions for me?"*

Best Practice: Always end the interview by thanking candidates for their interest in the position and for arranging their schedule to accommodate a full-day interview loop. And let them know what your time-frame is for making a decision.

PART SEVEN

HIRING GREAT PEOPLE –
TO HIRE OR NOT TO HIRE?

CHAPTER 32

TRY TO TALK THE CANDIDATE OUT OF THE JOB

(If You Want to Hire the Candidate)

If you're especially intrigued by a candidate and are thinking, "This is the person that I think I want to hire", try to talk the candidate out of the job.

"Huh? Jack, are you nuts?" Perhaps... but I'm quite serious. If your interview is going really well (and the previous interviews also went really well), it's very important to hold onto a *thread of skepticism* – to ensure that you and the other interviewers have not been mesmerized by a slick talker – before you make an offer.

If you are ready to make an offer on the spot, then you also need to test the candidate's resolve by *trying to talk the candidate out of the job* – and seeing how they react. You'll often learn a lot about the candidate by doing this. You will feel more confident in making an offer or you might sense that you are having second thoughts about whether this candidate is the right person for the job.

Tip: You need to determine whether the candidates are truly interested in your open position – or whether they are just trying to get an offer to wave in front of their current employer or the hiring manager in another company in order to try to get a better offer from them. When you try to talk candidates out of the job, they will not have a rehearsed response... and you might learn some interesting things about the candidate's character.

"How do I talk someone out of the job if I'm leaning toward hiring them?"
Here's how:

- Discuss the difficult aspects of the job. No sugar coatings. It's the right thing to do. It demonstrates to the candidate that you have integrity, value transparency, and want your team members to be realistic.
  - Tell them what's frustrating about working in your company.
  - Let them know that the decision-making processes can be frustrating.
  - Mention schedule pressures and budget headaches.
- Ask the candidate, *"What's your dream job 5 years from now?"*
  - If you have already asked this question, you can say, *"You said that your dream job was <xxx>."* And then ask the candidate...
  - *"Why not go after that type of job now?"* And then ask the candidate...
  - *"Why do you want* this *job?"*

The tactic of "talking them out of the job" is a way of testing whether the candidate is a good fit for your team culture and a good fit with you. As you try to talk them out of the job, you will learn:

- ... whether the candidate is comfortable with juggling multiple realities in multiple "time zones".
- ... whether the candidate is a realist who understands that no job is perfect – and that every job has its upsides and downsides (which speaks to the candidate's emotional maturity).
- ... how the candidate *feels about you* – because they are seeing and experiencing their potential manager in action, and that will influence their decision about whether this is a job they really want and a manager they really want to work for.

Caveat: Do *not* require or expect long-term loyalty. Doing so is ridiculous. *"Why?"* Because you might be leaving the company before the person you hire leaves the company (did that make you smile?)... and because people frequently change jobs (if possible under existing economic conditions) to seek new opportunities and/or more money or both.

If a potential Great Hire gives you a few highly-productive years, you'll be very happy because your team will prosper. That's a much better outcome than an OK Hire staying around for 10 years.

CHAPTER 33

TRUST YOUR GUT

At day's end you need to think about how you *feel* about the candidate's responses. Was the candidate forthcoming? Do you think that the candidate was honest? Did any of the candidate's responses make you tense or nervous? This is about *trusting your gut* more than your intellect.

> **Tip:** Your body doesn't lie. Your body will tell you how you truly feel about the candidate. That's the old brain at work, and it works at a faster speed than your new brain, which needs to figure things out to know what it thinks and believes. Trust your gut. It will seldom steer you wrong.

> **Caveat:** Your body *sometimes* can fool you. If a candidate reminds you of an old enemy or someone you dislike, you might not react well to the candidate. When you're having a negative reaction to a person, it's important to try to identify what's causing that reaction in you.

If you both feel comfortable with each other, there's a very good chance that things will work out well if you hire the candidate. If either you or the candidate does not feel comfortable, then it probably is not a match made in Heaven – and it's better to keep searching.

CHAPTER 34

GOING INTO "SELL" MODE

If the candidate is still interested in the job – i.e., if you have "failed" in your effort to talk the candidate out the job – and if you feel certain that this is the person that you want to hire and are therefore ready to make an offer on the spot (or ready to ask H.R. to extend an offer ASAP), then you can go into "sell" mode:

- Tell the candidate all the wonderful things about your team.
- Describe the candidate's future teammates.
- Summarize the team's current projects – and also mention upcoming projects (if you're not worried about letting out a company secret).
- Stress the types of job opportunities that could come up in the future.
- Mention training and other educational opportunities.
- Wax eloquently about the open-ended future of the company.

Best Practice: Be sure that some of your "sell points" are personal (not merely intellectual or factual): e.g., tell the candidate why you love your job, and why you love the team, and why you enjoy working at this company.

If you don't seem enthusiastic, why should the candidate be enthusiastic about joining your team?

CHAPTER 35

THE ROLE OF THE HIRING MANAGER

(That's You!)

You, as the Hiring Manager, are closely following the interview loop all day long, checking in regularly to read the feedback. After all, you are the Hiring Manager, and you to ensure that things are going smoothly. You need to study the Pros and Cons – and look long and hard at the comments about "Follow-up recommendations" and "Concerns" to see whether previous interviewers have addressed them at all or addressed them sufficiently.

You can also, at any point in the day, ask the next interviewer to follow-up on a particular concern.

Note: The "Concerns" and "Follow-up recommendations" noted by the second-to-last interviewer cannot be addressed by anyone except you – so you must decide whether you need to address them or whether you stick to the questions that you had planned to ask.)

Warning: *Do not send out your feedback to the other interviewers.* This is especially critical if there are internal candidates from other teams within the company or from your own team.

You make your decision and report it to H.R. and to your manager – or you meet with H.R. and your manager if you have concerns or questions.

Caveat: If a given candidate made a very good impression on you in almost all respects and also received "Hire" recommendations from everyone on the interview loop, but you find yourself hesitating to make an offer to the candidate, chances are there is something bothering you that you can't name and/or haven't figured out yet.

In such a case, do not make a hasty decision. Mull it over for a day... and you might figure out what's going on in your mind and your gut. (Yes, you might lose that candidate... and you'll never know whether that "loss" is a good thing or a bad thing: one of many difficult situations that go with the territory of being a manager.)

Often when you're feeling ambivalent, it's because you've picked up subtle signals that are putting you on edge – and it often isn't about the person's skillset or experience (because that would have been vetted both by H.R. and by you before an invitation to interview was sent – and then vetted again by the interviewers going on the loop before you). More likely it is something about the candidate's personality or body language or avoidance of eye contact while answering certain questions that is making you anxious about hiring that candidate. Try to get to the root of your anxiety by asking yourself questions such as:

- Is the candidate too slick?
- Is the candidate potentially high-maintenance?
- Is the candidate too egotistical, too self-centered, to be a good team fit?
- Is there something about the candidate's eye movements or body language that made you tense or distrustful at certain points during the interview? (Be aware that in some cultures people do not make eye contact when they speak.)
- Was there something about the candidate's tone of voice that made you think they were not truly that interested in the job or were not being fully transparent?
- Did the candidate try to take control (or succeed in taking control) of the interview?
- Did the candidate smile all the time, even when discussing serious matters? (Again, there are cultural differences about when or whether to smile... and a candidate might just be nervous.)

- Did the candidate indirectly say something about gender or culture or race that makes you concerned about the candidate's comfort level with diversity and ability to work well with others?
- Did you pick up on an inconsistency between what the candidate said about their work history and what is on the candidate's Resume?
- Did you pick up on some small inconsistency between what the candidate said to you and what the candidate said in an earlier interview?
- Did one of the other interviewer's comments make you anxious? (If "yes", you might want to chat with that interviewer in person to confirm what the intent of the comment was.)
- Are you concerned about whether the candidate has sufficient *upside potential*?

You might also want to have a few in-person conversations with other interviewers (after you have interviewed the candidate) to see whether they, too, picked up on something they couldn't or didn't articulate in their written feedback. You can ask them directly, *"Is this a person you want to work with? Is this a person you want on our team?"* Someone might say something that alleviates your concerns or that heightens them. Talking with and listening to others who interviewed the candidate can often be helpful in reaching a decision.

> **Best Practice:** It is helpful to get all the interviewers into the room for a debriefing that allows everyone to refine their thinking and artic-ulate additional reactions to each candidate. It also gives you a clear "read" on whether the team is excited about any of the candidates and whether there is agreement or disagreement among your Directs about the candidates.

If you're still on the fence, you should *not* hire the person. You should *always* feel excited, confident, and enthusiastic about onboarding a new person to your team. If you do not feel that way, that probably means the person is a "butt-in-seat hire" or a "Good Hire" – but not a Great Hire.

Difficult Dilemma: In corporate environments you sometimes get wind of coming headcount cuts or headcount freezes that will soon be announced. If you are desperate to have a position filled – particularly if a person has already left your team, and you are one person short, and there's just too much work for your team without another warm body – then you might decide to roll the dice on a Good Hire rather than roll the dice on losing the headcount if you hold out too long for a Great Hire.

Yes, a difficult dilemma. Sometimes it is better to have an almost-Great Hire than to be short a person, which could mean that everyone on your team will have to carry a heavier load for an indefinite time period – leading to burnout, stress, missed deadlines, and other undesirables (such as some of your Directs looking for other positions). That isn't good for your team as a whole, isn't good for the individuals on the team, isn't good for you, and probably isn't good for the company.

Note: Hiring an *almost*-Great Hire is not a sin. And sometimes that Good Hire turns out to be a Great Hire (just as a seeming Great Hire sometimes turns out to be a So-So Hire).

Why the Hiring Manager Goes Last in the Interview Loop

The Hiring Manager should always go last in an interview loop, but rare occasions do arise when the Hiring Manager cannot be the last interviewer. For example, the Hiring Manager might have a critical meeting that was scheduled on short notice at the end of that day and therefore has to interview the candidate earlier in the loop.

That said, every effort should be made – and I mean *every* effort – to have the Hiring Manager go last, even if it means doing the interview at an unconventional time. For example:

- If you are free that evening, arrange a post-dinner interview with the candidate. (This assumes that the candidate is not flying home that evening.)

- If you and the candidate are available early the next morning, reschedule the interview. (This assumes that the candidate does not need to catch an airplane early the next morning.)

If there really is no way for the Hiring Manager (you!) to go last in the loop, then you have these options to choose from:

- Ask your own manager to sit in as the wrap-up interviewer. (And if your manager cannot be your proxy, perhaps your skip-level manager can do the wrap-up interview.)
- Select the most senior and experienced interviewer from among your Direct Reports to be your proxy in an emergency. You can train them by doing the following:
  - Coach that person on what their role is as the final interviewer (well before the need ever arises).
  - Let that person be a silent observer at one or two of your final interviews, so they can observe how you fulfill your role and are therefore better prepared to be your proxy.
  - After your proxy-designate observes you doing one or two final interviews, you should do a post-mortem with the observer after each interview so that the person can ask you questions and so that you can assess how well the lessons are being absorbed. Ask the proxy-designate for their "take" on the candidate... before you give your "take" on the candidate.
  - Arrange a "dress rehearsal" (mock interview) so that you can observe how prepared your proxy-designate is to be your stand-in.

CHAPTER 36

THE "CHAMELEON CANDIDATE" NIGHTMARE

(or: the Tale of a Bad Hire)

The "Chameleon Candidate" is a person who instantly and intuitively psyches out what the interviewer is looking for in a response. They do not merely lie (which anyone can do). They have an uncanny and mind-boggling ability to say exactly what the interviewer wants to hear. Think of those rare people who are idiot savants and can multiply two 12-digit numbers in their head in seconds: the Chameleon Candidate can perform another type of "magic", but in the interview arena.

Let me tell you a true-life story...

Years ago I managed a large webteam at a multi-national tech company. The webteam was responsible for creating, maintaining, and evolving over 90 public-facing product websites. I recall a time when one of the product websites was in need of a producer – someone who could take text and images provided by a product marketing manager or a technical program manager and recast the text so that it would be appropriate for our audiences. This required certain skills and experience – e.g., a working knowledge of HTML and some editorial chops in order to post the new text and images in the right place while removing whatever text or images were no longer needed.

About 60 people applied for this position. H.R. screened the Resumes, did about 15 telephone screens, and cut the list down to the 8 or 9 most-promising applicants. I then reviewed those applications, and asked H.R. to bring in 4 people for full-day interview loops.

As the interview loops proceeded and the interviewers provided real-time feedback, one candidate was getting unanimous rave reviews from everyone… with unanimous "Hire" recommendations.

I was *not* the Hiring Manager: one of my Direct Reports was the Hiring Manager. I went last on the interview loop because the Hiring Manager was not very experienced at hiring, so I was the safety net. Although all 4 candidates did well in the loop, this one candidate was an extra-special shining star – in skills, experience, and team fit. Seemingly, this candidate was going to be the one to hire – unless I found some fatal flaw during my interview with him.

My interview with the candidate went well – and I agreed with the Hiring Manager's desire to hire this candidate. We both felt confident that he was the Great Hire that we were looking for – and that we needed to grab him before some other company or internally-competing unit did. (The candidate was doing interview loops with two other teams in our company.)

We hired him!

This new-hire producer showed up for work about 3 weeks later. The first day was taken up with corporate orientation, as was the norm. He reported to my unit the next day, and I heard through the grapevine that he seemed to be struggling. I brushed it off as a break-in period.

His manager (who reported to me) came to my office on Day 3 of the new hire's arrival and said something along the lines of: *"He doesn't know how to do any of the things that we need him to do."* I asked: "Are you saying that he doesn't have the producer skills that he said he had?" The manager said, *"Yeah, that's what I'm saying. He can't do even the most basic things that he said he could do. His resume is bullshit."*

I asked, "Is someone working side-by-side with him to try to teach him how we do things?" And the manager said, *"Of course. But he doesn't know*

HTML, and he said he did. He can't edit worth a damn, doesn't know editorial mark-up shorthand, isn't familiar with the Chicago Manual of Style. He said he had lots of experience writing and editing – but he doesn't. This is a disaster! What do we do?"

I asked, "Is there anything that you'd like me to do?" And the manager said, *"Would you talk to him, push hard, and tell me whether you agree that we need to get rid of him?"* I said, "Please give it one more day… and watch closely what's going – and then get back to me late today or early tomorrow morning. If something doesn't change significantly by this afternoon, I'll deal with it tomorrow."

The Hiring Manager came to me at the end of the Day 3 and said, *"Nothing's changed. He can't do the job. Please, please, please do something about this."*

Note: Normally I would leave it to the Hiring Manager to deal with personnel issues. ("It's your new hire. You take care of it.") However, in this case the Hiring Manager was a fairly recent hire with zero experience in dealing with delicate personnel matters. Because of the potential H.R. and Legal complications, the Hiring Manager and H.R. and I met to discuss the situation. The Hiring Manager and H.R. both thought it best if I stepped in to deal with the situation… and I did.

I met with the new-hire producer the next morning – his Day 4 on the job. I was direct – not brusque or impolite, but straightforward, even-toned, and calm. I started off by saying, "It doesn't seem to be working out. Would you agree?"

He nodded his head slowly and said, *"Yeah, it's been rough."*

I said, "On your resume it says that you know HTML coding language, and you said so in your interviews – but you don't seem to know HTML. Is that right?"

Again, he nodded: *"I thought I could learn it really fast if someone coached me."*

I said, "Your resume shows that you have editing experience, but your manager says that you don't know how to mark up a manuscript. Is that correct?"

Again he nodded, but didn't say anything immediately... and then, after a long pause, he said, *"I really love the Web, and this is a great company – so I really wanted to work here and get in on the ground floor."*

I said, "I'm sorry, but this isn't going to work out."

Tip: If you are ever in a similar situation as a Hiring Manager, resist the strong urge to get angry at the candidate for lying and wasting a lot of the company's time money. Also resist the strong urge you might have to be sympathetic and parental. You are *not* responsible for the mess that this person is in. He lied, and that's what caused the mess. You are responsible only for cleaning up the mess as quickly and cleanly as possible.

I then said, "We have two options. You can resign immediately, or I will contact H.R. and ask them to begin formal dismissal procedures. How would you like to handle it?"

He said, *"I'll resign."*

And I said, "I'll let H.R. and your manager know what's happening. Go back to your office for now. Someone from H.R. will contact you today, and you'll be asked to go to the H.R. office to fill out the official resignation documents."

End of story... except that you're probably thinking, *"What the heck happened? How did things go so terribly wrong? How did everyone get fooled?"* Here's what happened...

This candidate was more than a skilled liar. This person was a perfect example of the Chameleon Candidate, one of those rare people who knows instinctively what a given interviewer wants to hear – and changes "colors" as easily as a chameleon does. Tripping up a skilled liar in an interview loop is doable. Tripping up a Chameleon Candidate can be very difficult.

It also helped that he was articulate, nicely dressed, good-looking, earnest, convincing, had a killer smile, and had a flawless resume (which he largely fabricated and probably had someone edit for him). This Chameleon's ability to provide an answer in words that each interviewer wanted to hear was uncanny... and he fooled me, and fooled all the other interviewers. So what could we have done differently? Read on...

How to Prevent It from Happening Again

Perhaps you're asking yourself, *"How do I protect myself from a Chameleon Candidate?"* That's precisely what I asked myself after this fiasco.

I came up with a two-prong line of defense, and my teams never again hired a Chameleon Candidate (and that record encompasses 12 years and more than 300 candidates who came through interview loops). Yes, there were other Chameleon Candidates, but they were unmasked by adding two procedures to what became our standard interview protocol:

- **Joint Interview (two interviewers)** – Always have at least one in-office interview conducted by two interviewers who have different personalities and different skill-sets. *"Why two?"* Because Chameleon Candidates instinctively know what one person wants to hear, but if you put a Chameleon Candidate in a situation in which they have to triangulate between two people, their game is up: they can't please and psyche out two different of people at the same time. Check-mate.
- **Lunch Interview (with two or more interviewers)** – Take the Chameleon Candidate to lunch, preferably in a noisy company cafeteria or restaurant. A company cafeteria or crowded restaurant creates distractions and noise – and selecting food and cutting/eating food requires focus – all of which makes it more difficult for the Chameleon Candidate to focus solely on the interviewers and provide the perfect responses. Although the Chameleon Candidate has an amazing ability to know instantaneously what each interviewer wants to hear, that ability is undermined when faced with two or more people (who might want to hear different things). Again, check-mate.

Best Practice: The joint-interview technique is very useful for interviewing all finalists for a position. Joint interviews should be conducted before the Hiring Manager's interview.

All candidates try to do a little "spinning" – and some try to take control of the interview – even if they are not a Chameleon Candidate. You never know, until it's too late, whether a given candidate is a Chameleon or just good at "spinning", which is why you need to employ this Best Practice with all candidates. (The only exceptions are internal candidates who are known to be non-Chameleons).

Additional Benefit of Joint Interviews: If you pair up an experienced interviewer and a less-experienced interviewer (as mentioned earlier), you create an on-the-job training opportunity for less-experienced interviewers to enhance their interviewing skills.

CHAPTER 37

Beware "the Passion Thing"

Everyone seems to be talking about "passion for the job" and "passion for the industry" when thinking about hiring. It's all over the Internet and in print interviews with CEOs and in articles by management gurus: The message almost always seems to be: "Look for someone with a lot of passion... and hire that person" – and it often sounds as though that's the top-of-mind criterion, the critical factor in deciding whether to hire someone.

It shouldn't be. I think that there is a serious over-emphasis on "passion", that too much reliance is being placed on that trait.

Trying to assess the future performance of a candidate is much more difficult and complex than deciding whether the candidate is sufficiently passionate or the most-passionate candidate. And what is "passion" anyways? Is *enthusiasm* or *excitement* or *intensity* somehow being measured? If 'yes', *how* is it being measured?

Note: This chapter discusses *expressed* passion – not *inner* passion. Expressed passion can be real or faked.

There are *three potential problems* with basing hiring decisions largely on whether a candidate is sufficiently passionate.

Problem #1 – Rehearsed Passion

If the candidates have done their homework (and most finalists will have), they have read all about Hiring Managers looking for a passionate candidate. *So what do you think they do as part of their preparation for an interview loop?* They practice exuding passion, of course. The job is delicious ice cream, and passion is the hot fudge that they pour on top of the ice cream.

Some candidates will be better thespians than others – but is it your goal to hire the best thespian? (I hope not... unless you're hiring someone for a sales position, in which case dramatic skills can come in handy.)

Remember: The degree of passion tells you very little about how well a candidate will perform on the job.

Problem #2 – Cultural and Personality Differences

Some cultures and some individuals are passionate about everything – big and small, work-related or not work-related. You name it – music, a weed peeking up through a crack in the cement sidewalk, children, video games, a favorite sports team, a delicious recipe, the color of a flower in Spring – passionate, passionate, passionate. So if a candidate comes from a passionate culture or just has a passionate personality – and talks excitedly and waves their arms – they will be oh-so-passionate about the job you need to fill. So their degree of passion tells you *nothing* as an indicator of future performance.

The reverse is true in other cultures, where it is considered improper or rude or immature or unpleasantly aggressive to exhibit emotion. Such cultures place a high value on calm and composure and politeness – not on exhibiting emotion. If candidates are from such cultures, and if you dismiss them out of hand or are less impressed by them and are reluctant to hire them because of what you judge to be insufficient passion, you will be overlooking some potentially Great Hires.

Problem #3 – The Double-Bind of Women Candidates

Professional women are often in a "can't win" situation: if they *do* exhibit passion, they might be stereotyped as emotional: e.g., "high maintenance" or "not tough enough" or "not a rational problem-solver". And if they do *not* exhibit passion, they might be stereotyped as "rational" or "aggressive" or "a cold fish" or "distant".

Ergo, the highly accomplished female candidate has to be more careful than a male candidate about the passion thing. Female candidates need to decide how to play it – and it can be a very difficult choice for them. Yes, the context matters: e.g., perhaps more exhibited passion for sales and marketing positions, perhaps less exhibited passion for a developer (programmer) or financial-analyst position. These are, of course, gross generalizations… but you get the idea.

You, as the Hiring Manager, need to be aware of the double-bind that women candidates sometimes find themselves in – and you should therefore largely disregard the passion thing and instead focus on the fundamentals (skills, experience, team fit, and so on)… or you risk letting some Great Hires elude you.

Additional Thoughts on Passion

Of the hundreds of interview loops that I've participated in, I have *not* seen a marked passion-index difference between hires that have worked out well and hires that have not worked out well. If anything, I would say that a higher percentage of "high passion" candidates did *not* work out in comparison to "medium-to-low passion" candidates.

"How could that be?" I think the likeliest answer is that it's often easier to like and be "seduced" by high-passion types than by low-passion types. Low-passion and medium-passion candidates must really be extra-impressive in other ways – e.g., very high I.Q., a very special skillset, unique experience – for a Hiring Manager to roll the dice on the less-passionate candidates.

Caveat: Passion is, in the history of humankind, closely associated with seduction. In the interview setting, the question is: *"Who is seducing whom?"*

Different people can have very different motivations. My hard-won conclusion is that a person's motivations, talent, relevant experience, and perseverance are what determine success or failure on the job.

You've probably heard the expression "When the going gets tough, the tough get going." If I were faced with two candidates who were roughly equivalent in education, technical skills, collaborative skills, creativity, and experience, with the exceptions that one candidate ranked very high on the passion scale and the other candidate ranked very high on the mental toughness scale, I'd pick the mentally tough candidate every time.

"Why?" Because every business has its ups and downs – and in bad times I'd prefer to be working side-by-side with people who are grounded and tough-minded rather than working with people who are passionate, and perhaps mercurial, and who crash when tough realities bring them down to Earth.

That said, if you find mental toughness and passion in one person, think seriously about hiring that person ASAP!

Moral of the story: Do not be fooled or overly-influenced by the presence of passion… or its absence. It's a teensy part of the whole picture.

A Hiring Manager's perception and subsequent subjective "rating" of passion is akin to mind-reading – so I don't give it too much weight. (Yeah, you can give it a *little* weight.)

CHAPTER 38

Instant Prejudice

We all form opinions quickly. Much research has corroborated that first impressions matter and stick in our minds... and are usually correct. Most managers that I've discussed this with say that, within the first 5 minutes of a 60-minute interview, they know whether or not they are going to hire the candidate. I've also found that to be true, but...

I have on more than a few occasions decided "no hire" within the first 5 minutes of an interview – and then was surprised as my opinion changed as the interview went on. What made me change my mind?

I changed my mind because, as the interview progressed, more of the candidate's character "emerged". *"Why did that happen?"* Here are some possible explanations:

- Perhaps the candidate was very nervous, and it took a while for the candidate to calm down and settle into a rhythm.
- Perhaps my first few questions were unintentionally confusing or inappropriate in some way that I wasn't aware of... but the candidate perked up as the interview continued.
- Perhaps the candidate was having a late-afternoon energy low, and caught a second wind. (All-day interview loops are tiring, especially if the candidate has traveled a long ways to get to your company... and might be jet-lagged.)
- Perhaps the previous interviewer had said some things that were improper or insulting or confusing... and the candidate was still reacting to that.

- Perhaps the candidate had checked email between interviews and just learned that a relative or an old friend had died.

You might be thinking, *"So what? I want someone on my team who is not thrown by any challenging situations, who can perform at a high level under all circumstances."* That's a reasonable thought to have and a sensible way to feel. I've occasionally had the same thought. That said…

First impressions can be wrong. Not often, perhaps, but it does happen occasionally. Your role is to be a professional interviewer. Do not give up on a candidate in the first 5 minutes because you feel certain that the candidate is a "no hire". Once in a while an interview will take an unexpected turn, and you'll end up thinking that the person is actually a strong candidate. You might even hire that candidate – and be glad that you did.

Caveat: Remember that it's a small world – and within an industry vertical, it can be a *very* small world. Every candidate might know people who at some future date might want to apply for a job in your company and even on your team. You don't want that "unimpressive" candidate to spread the word that the Hiring Manager treated them poorly. That could result in future Great Hires not applying for positions on your team. That's a really bad unintended consequence – which you have the power to prevent.

So even if your first "take" on a candidate is negative and that "take" doesn't change by the end of the interview, it's still very important to maintain your professionalism by treating that candidate as well as you would treat a candidate in whom you're interested.

CHAPTER 39

HIRE PEOPLE WHO ARE SMARTER THAN YOU

"Why would I want to do that? I'm the manager because I'm smarter and know more than my Direct Reports do? That's why I got the job."

Some managers think that they have to be the smartest person on the team – or they won't be respected by their Direct Reports. That is not the case. Your team wants you to be a very competent manager and a great leader – i.e., a Great Manager, who is widely respected and influential, and who provides guidance and opportunity without micro-managing. Though your Directs won't use this terminology, what they want is for you to *create conditions that make it possible for them to succeed.*

If you are the "smartest" person on the team (by your judgment), then you will always be frustrated because your Directs will never be able to match your standards or abilities (let alone exceed them). Yes, you *are* allowed to be smartest in *some* ways… but don't get delusional about how wonderful you are and how smart you are in *every* way.

An important aspect of your job is to build a Great Team – and have your team demonstrate continuous improvement. To accomplish those goals, every new hire – whether a replacement hire or a new-headcount hire – must have *some* unique experience and/or industry knowledge and/or skillset that is different from your own – and different from anyone else on your team. That's how you raise the bar to develop a higher-performance team. Yes, I'm talking about a *value-add hire*. If you hire someone who is just good enough to keep the trains running, that will not improve your team's performance or your credibility rating in the eyes of peers and upper management.

A corollary to a *value-add hire* is: *Hire for potential.* You always want your team to get better, to get smarter, to grow, to take on more responsibility, to innovate, to increase efficiency – so you need to be hiring for *upside potential*. You want each new hire to contribute to taking your team to the mountaintop.

Remember: Great Hires are a requirement for building a Great Team.

You can't be best at everything. And if you were promoted from within your team to become the new manager, you need to have Direct Reports who are as good as you (or, preferably, better than you) at what you used to do when you were a full-time sole contributor.

When a new, really smart, experienced, skilled person who desires to excel joins your team, everyone on the team takes notice... and it ups their game. *"Why?"* Because competitive juices begin to stir when the new kid on the block arrives and shines. The new Great Hire helps prevent your Direct Reports from becoming complacent and staying in the "keep the trains running" mode. The new Great Hire rapidly shifts the rest of your team into the "how can we do this better, faster, cheaper, smarter" mode.

PART EIGHT

ADDRESSING PERSONNEL PROBLEMS

CHAPTER 40

RETAINING STAFF

(or Letting Them Go Gracefully)

"To retain or not to retain: that is the question."

Do you have a Direct Report who is thinking about leaving your team? Is that person a high performer, someone that you will want to do everything *reasonably possible* to convince that person to remain on the team?

Caveat: Don't make promises you can't keep in order to keep someone on your team. Desperate actions later lead to serious regrets – at work and in other aspects of one's life – and you can't rerun the Desperate Acts "video" to create a new ending.

Tip: Retaining staff *must be* an ongoing activity – an *everyday activity*. If you wait to shift into high gear to retain someone, it's often too late... because by the time that you're aware of the Direct Report's desire to be moving on, that person has probably already begun looking for another position. Usually a Direct Report's thoughts about leaving the team have almost certainly been brewing for some time – and it's difficult to reverse the momentum.

Others on the team might already know the person is looking, which also makes it difficult for the person to come back into the fold... because certain intra-team dynamics have already been set in motion – out of your view.

Note to New Managers: People who have been unhappy might view the arrival of a new manager as a fresh start – or they often begin "looking around" for another job when there is a change of manager.

Happy campers might also look around if they had a great relationship with the manager who came before you and figure that they had a good run and should move on – and they might even try to follow that manager to that manager's next watering hole.

Whichever the case, don't take it personally: this "looking around" dynamic comes with the "new manager" territory... and is normal.

It can be difficult to discern which of your Directs Reports might be looking for another position: after all, you're the new manager, so everyone on your team is going to be polite – and guarded. Ergo, you should assume that *you need to be in retention mode from the moment you walk in* as the new manager.

Whether you are a new manager of the team or the veteran manager of a team, you'll *see* the early warning signs of "looking around" if you're alert. Sometimes you'll just have a *feeling*... but aren't sure what's changed or what's wrong. When you get such a feeling about one of your Directs, this thought should immediately pop into your mind: "Uh-oh, they're thinking about leaving." You will need to decide whether you want to retain that person... or whether you view that person's leaving as an opportunity to hire a new person and raise the quality bar of your team.

Early Warning Signs

Fortunately, you can do a number of things to increase the likelihood of picking up on the "early warning signs" of a Direct Report who is thinking about leaving your team.

"What are some of the symptoms of unhappiness or restlessness?" Here are a few telling symptoms of "disengagement" of a Direct Report:

- Seems less focused than before.

- "Spaces out" more frequently than before.
- Smiles or laughs less often than before.
- Doesn't go to lunch with teammates as often as before.
- Starts showing up late for work or for team meetings.
- Takes more sick days than previously (perhaps to interview elsewhere).
- Doesn't volunteer for anything (and they used to "step up"); just keeps the trains running.
- Speaks up less at team meetings… or says less when they do speak up – and with less energy.

Retention Strategies

The following approaches can help with retention of your Direct Reports:

- ***Try to figure out the source of the unhappiness or restlessness.***
  If you observe or feel you are "picking up on" unhappiness or restlessness, act on your instincts. It might be that your Direct Report is unhappy with their work situation… so ask them directly: "Is there something going on that's bothering you?" Or: "Is there anything that I can help with?"

  - If there *is* something bothering them at work, they'll likely fess up – and you can work with them to improve the situation.
  - If something is bothering them *outside* of work, they might tell you that, though they might not offer the specifics. (You don't need to know the specifics… but some Directs might say what's up – illness in the family, relationship issues, financial concerns, etc. – and doing so might help them to relax to get it out in the open and makes it possible for them to re-focus on work.)

- ***Schedule a "Stay" interview (but don't call it that) with each of your Direct Reports within 1 month of your arrival on the scene.***
  If a person has been on your team 1 year or more (independent of whether you have been their manager for 1 year or more), you should have a frank discussion about what s-he wants to do next in their career move and how s-he envisions their career long-term. You do

this by asking directly: *"What do you want to do next?"* And when you hear the response, ask: *"What's your time frame?"* Or ask: *"What do you want to be doing 5 years from now?"*

Yeah, get it all out in the open. If you've never done this before, it will take some getting used to... but you'll love the results of these conversations, which often aide in retention. The answers to these questions will give you valuable clues about whether your Direct Reports' current responsibilities are on the path to what they want to be doing in 5 years. Think about whether there are ways that you can help them reach their 5-year goal... because that's good both for your team (helps with retention) and for them (prepares them for their next position).

- Sometimes, especially the first time you ask such questions, you might be met with stunned silence – because your Direct Report has never had a manager who had such a candid conversation with them.
- And sometimes they'll simply say, "I haven't thought about it. I'm happy where I am, doing what I'm doing." (That might or might not be true)
- By having such conversations with your Directs every 6 months, they get used to it (and you get better at it)... and they begin thinking more about their careers (especially if they're relative "youngsters").

  As you and they gradually become more comfortable with these discussions, you'll be on the way to creating a culture of respect, nurturance, transparency, and encouragement – viz., a Great Team Culture. When you accomplish that, people will almost always walk the extra mile for you and for the team – and if they need to move on, they will give you lots of advance notice, so they don't create problems with a sudden exit.

  Note: You will not lose your Direct Reports by encouraging them to think about their careers beyond their time on your team. In my experience, the reverse happens – because they see you not only as their manager but also as mentor and coach… and that, paradoxically, makes them want to stay around longer.

- **Schedule a semi-annual 1-to-1 meeting to identify current interests and energy level.** *(This meeting is not the recurring weekly 1-to-1… but it could be combined with the semi-annual career-discussion meeting.)*

This meeting will help you to ascertain what your Direct Reports would like to accomplish on your team… and afterward. You will pick up clues about how each of your Directs is doing emotionally… if you *listen* and *ask the right questions*. If your Direct Reports' current responsibilities do not align with their 5-year trajectory, you have three choices:

  ○ Give your Directs a business-relevant stretch goal that aligns with their "next career step".
  ○ Give your Directs permission to do a side project that will allow them to develop skills and experience that align with their 5-year trajectory. (You'll be amazed at how often doing this will totally re-energize a Direct, especially a Direct who likes being on your team and would prefer to not leave.)
  ○ Work with your Directs to find appropriate training courses.

Note: You want each of your Direct Reports to perceive you as a manager who wants to *help them further their careers* (rather than entrap them).

Career planning with your Directs in an open and encouraging manner is a great way to demonstrate that you that you not only talk the talk… but that you walk the walk. They will appreciate that you have their best long-term interests at heart – and that is part of building a Great Team Culture.

Remember: If a Direct Report is merely "hanging around" while they are secretly looking for another position, s-he will leak energy and increasingly lose interest – and that will have a negative effect on your team's morale and on productivity. Better to face up to the reality – and solve the problem sooner rather than later.

If It Isn't a Fit, Let Them Go Gracefully

If the circumstances on your team and the needs of your team are not a fit for restless Direct Reports, *let them go gracefully*. It's the right thing to do. Your team will see that you have not maligned or punished the "deserter", and that's important.

If the right position for this person does not exist within your company, offer to brainstorm with them how they might go about getting the type of position they desire, offer to review their Resume, and offer to be a reference (if they are a top performer). Your soon-to-be ex-Direct Report will appreciate this enormously – and you'll feel like you've done the right thing as a manager and as a person. And others on your team will learn (because nothing within a team is ever secret for long) that you took the high road – and their appreciation of you as a manager will increase, which will increase loyalty and aide retention.

Best Practice: If the Direct Report is a Great Hire – but they need to leave your team for career-development reasons – help them find a job somewhere else *in your company*. You do not want to lose Great Hires to the competition. It's much better to retain a Great Hire within your company than to have a Great Hire walk out the door to a competitor.

CHAPTER 41

DEALING WITH BAD APPLES

You can't let Bad Apples continue to behave badly. You either need to devise a rehabilitation program for the Bad Apple or you need to get rid of the Bad Apple. If you don't do either of these, hoping naively that the problem will go away or miraculously improve by itself, you are in danger of losing your team because they will view you as incompetent or cowardly.

An experienced manager can tell you that one Bad Apple on a team can make life miserable for everyone on the team – including the manager (you!).

Warning: If you have *two* Bad Apples on your team, that's a very serious problem – as in *urgent*. Fixing both situations is really tough… though sometimes if you fix one, the other self-corrects. (That might sound like wishful thinking, but I've seen it happen. *Why?* Because the two Bad Apples often feed off of and embolden each other.)

Often the best strategy is to focus on the Bad Apple who seems most redeemable. If you can convert that Bad Apple into an OK Apple or a Good Apple, that's goodness. Then focus on the second Bad Apple – who will have noticed the change and will either begin changing her/himself or be looking for another position.

If you cannot turn around the situation with one or both of the Bad Apples, then the handwriting is on the wall. Fix the situation sooner rather than later. The longer you delay, the worse the situation will become.

How Do You Identify a Bad Apple?

Not too difficult a task. Here are some common traits of Bad Apples:

- Is a loud-mouth and tries to dominate meetings.
- Is unpleasantly argumentative.
- Won't share work in progress that is part of a collaborative team effort.
- Gets angry easily and quickly, out of proportion to the situation.
- Becomes frustrated way more often than other team members.
- Is passive-aggressive, sarcastic, or insulting.
- Withdraws from participating whenever the team doesn't agree with her/him.
- Talks behind people's backs.
- Complains a lot.
- Is a poor listener and is not responsive to what others have said.
- Repeatedly asks for special treatment.
- Unjustly accuses the manager of favoritism.
- Is competitive in an unhealthy way.
- Feedback offered is 75% negative and 25% positive (i.e., constructive).
- Seldom likes the assignments given to them.
- Thinks they are smarter than everyone – and are not bashful about saying so.
- Sends out irritating or attacking emails.
- Puts down others to make themselves look better.
- Is verbally abusive.

Can You Fix the Situation?

Probably not. But it's worth a try. If you and your manager want to give it a go, it will take a coordinated effort, sometimes with H.R.'s help (and, if necessary, with Legal weighing in).

Usually retention is considered for a Bad Apple only if the person brings something of unique value to the company's success. As you consider whether to try to fix the situation, you will need to ask yourself these questions:

- *"Do I want to try to retain the Direct Report? Or do I view the situation as unfixable?"*
- If the Direct does have a unique skillset, is it possible to isolate the person as a sole contributor so that interaction with the team or other units is minimized?
- Has the person always behaved this way? If 'yes', it's probably an uphill battle to improve the situation. If 'no', then find out the answers to these questions:
  - Who was the Hiring Manager who brought the Bad Apple into the company? (Hopefully, it wasn't your current manager or skip-level manager.)
  - Why hasn't anyone addressed the bad behavior before?
  - If the bad behavior was addressed before, by whom? in what ways? and what was the outcome?
  - Were the Direct Report's bad traits mentioned in past performance reviews?

If you have discussed the situation with your manager and H.R., and if you all agree that the situation can't be fixed despite your best efforts, and if you haven't had to deal with a termination situation before, talk to your manager and H.R. about the termination procedure. (H.R. will involve Legal if necessary.)

CHAPTER 42

TEAM DESTROYERS – THE "GREATS"

Managers sometimes have to deal with seriously difficult people. Such people come in many stripes, but I'll focus on what some people would call "egoists" or "narcissists" who exhibit delusions of grandeur.

The term *narcissist*, in its nontechnical every-day usage, conjures up someone who looks in the mirror and is very pleased with the reflection – an altogether wonderful example of the human species. The term *narcissist* is also a term of art in the field of psychology – and it has deeper meanings.

I am not a psychologist, so my use of the term *narcissist* is not based on expert psychological knowledge. But I have seen certain traits that lend themselves to the common (nontechnical) meaning of the word "narcissist" – and those traits can cause huge problems for a manager, a team, and a business.

It's time for two true-life stories...

Meet "Martha the Great"

Martha (not her real name) was well-liked by those who knew her casually. She was intelligent, and she generally did her work well when her manager channeled her energy. I was her skip-level manager.

Martha thought she got along well with her manager – a view not shared by her manager, who had told me a number of times that Martha required a lot of hand-holding because she would space out, go off in various directions, and work on things other than her assignments.

Martha would drop by my office a couple of times a week and, standing by the open door to my office, say: *"Got a minute?"* I usually said "Sure", and she would sit down and start telling me about her latest ideas. They were often quite interesting and unusual; however, they usually had little or nothing to do with the business we were in or the goals that our team was trying to achieve. So I would often say something like, "That's really interesting. Unfortunately, that doesn't have anything to with this team's charter."

Martha's manager began to complain that Martha was spending more time on her self-invented side projects than on the projects assigned to her. She delivered her projects on time only about 50% to 75% of the time, though they usually met or exceeded the quality bar. Other people on the team became disgruntled because they felt that management was playing favorites and allowing Martha to work on whatever project she wanted to work on.

Clearly, we had a problem (actually, three problems): with Martha, with team morale, and with Martha's manager. It became clear that Martha the Great felt that she was a gift to the universe, that she was smarter and more creative than everyone, and that she should be allowed to do whatever she wanted to do. It was clear to me that this situation could not be endured much longer.

I had some long conversations with Martha's manager, who was fairly new as a manager, about how to handle the situation. We also met with an experienced H.R. person to get her views on how best to proceed.

To make a long story short, Martha's manager and I jointly met with Martha and gently and firmly laid out the options:

- If Martha was to stay on the team, she had to make the team's strategies and goals her main focus.
- If Martha was unwilling or unable to do that, she would need to find another job, perhaps on an R&D team within our company or in another company.

Martha said she would think about it and get back to us within a few days. We learned from other sources that she immediately began to look for another job. When we met with her a few days later, Martha said, "You're right. I need to find another job where I can work on the things that I like to work on."

Within a month Martha had found her dream job in another corner of the company. We parted ways on friendly terms, and we wished her well. Team morale quickly bounced back to its former high level.

About 6 months later, I heard through the grapevine that Martha had left the company. I don't know whether her leaving was voluntary, though I was not surprised that Martha the Great had moved on.

Meet "Sheldon the Great"

Sheldon (not his real name) was in charge of a product website and managed a small team. He was intelligent and experienced. I was his skip-level manager.

A set of issues arose among my team – concerning a confusing customer online experience across dozens of websites. The issues needed to be decided in a manner that would work across all of the company's product websites. Having a single common code base (instead of seven code bases) to maintain and evolve and having a unified design (instead of more than a dozen designs with different navigation schemes) would make it far easier to roll out new features far more quickly. It would also create a unified, coherent customer experience: if customers knew how to navigate one product website, they would know how to navigate all the product websites.

I scheduled a 4-hour off-site meeting to discuss all the issues with the "players" from different teams – program management, product management, information architecture, editorial, marketing, graphic design, coding, and test. Key representatives from each area – a manager and one or two front-line staffers from each group – were invited to help resolve the complex multi-layered issues, thus avoiding a series of separate meetings and endless email exchanges. The objective of the meeting was to get buy-in from all the groups on a set of uniform solutions.

The meeting went well. Yes, there was plenty of heated debate, but also a lot of give and take and compromise… and, finally, consensus emerged on the major issues because everyone in the room maintained their focus on the end-user experience rather than on their fiefdom. When I adjourned the meeting, everyone knew the plan, and everyone was on board to develop detailed specifications and then to implement the changes.

Two days later, Sheldon's manager walks into my office and says, *"Sheldon isn't following the specs that we all agreed on."*

"Did you ask him why he wasn't sticking to the action plan that we all agreed on?"

"Yes", she said. (long pause) *"You know what he said?"* (pause) *"He said, 'I don't like what everyone agreed to do. I think that what I'm doing is better.' What am I supposed to do? I've never dealt with anything like this."*

I told her to start documenting the ways in which Sheldon was not following the agreed-upon plan – and to write up as-close-to-verbatim notes as possible of any conversations she had with him… and to send them to me ASAP. I also offered to talk to Sheldon. My Direct Report Manager said, *"Yes, puh-leez."*

Note: Sheldon's manager – my Direct Report – had never dealt with this type of employee. Usually I would not jump in to rescue one of my managers, but I didn't have a good feeling about this situation, and my Direct was asking for help. I conferred with H.R., and H.R. agreed that it would be good if I met with Sheldon alone to verify what my newbie Direct Report Manager had described to me.

Sheldon came into my office that afternoon. I asked him whether he thought it was OK to not follow specs that were developed by and signed off on by the entire team, and he said, *"I think you all made a bad decision"*. I asked him why he had not conformed to the agreed-upon specifications. He said, *"I don't like the specs. My website looks better."*

I didn't bother asking him about the disjointed customer experience that would result from a nonconforming website because his tone and body language had made it clear to me that Sheldon didn't give a hoot about anything other than his little corner of the world. I simply told him, politely, that if he didn't adhere to agreed-upon specifications, that I would have to find someone who would. He didn't look happy, but he got the message.

Sheldon reluctantly began to implement the new design specifications. He would appear in my office every few days, tell me how lousy his manager was, and that if I were a competent manager, I would get rid of his manager and make him the manager. (I am *not* making this up.)

Three weeks later, Sheldon the Great informed us that he had gotten a job at another company and was resigning. The people in our team's hallways breathed a sigh of relief.

CHAPTER 43

How to SMARTly Manage a Martha or a Sheldon... or Worse

You might inherit a "high maintenance" Direct Report like a Martha or Sheldon... or worse.

"What's the optimal way for me to manage a very difficult person?"

One approach that has worked well for me in setting expectations is making use of the SMART goals protocol.

SMART Goals (an Excellent Methodology for All Your Direct Reports)

SMART goals are not my invention – and are defined somewhat differently by different sources. That said, here are the term definitions for the SMART acronym that I have found to be most useful:

Specific	Precise, detailed description of each task/project.
Measurable	Methods for measuring quality, quantity, and timeliness are specified.
Achievable	Task is doable and is realistic given the deadline for completion (if the project is a far-out, far-reaching, visionary project with many unknowns, then the SMART framework might not be appropriate).
Relevant	Task is aligned with Vision, Mission, and Goals – and customers (external and internal) need this done.
Time-delimited	Defined schedule of development phases, with a deadline for completion of work. (The manager and the Direct Report must discuss and agree on the time line.)

Caveat: Be sure that you set annual SMART goals for *all* your Direct Reports. Doing so is especially useful (as in, mandatory and critical) when managing a difficult person – because you can't discriminate: if it's a necessity for managing one of your Direct Reports, then it's a must-do for all your Directs. Having a SMART framework eliminates most gray areas, misunderstandings, and later finger-pointing.

Best Practice: When you give out a new assignment to a Direct Report, be sure to discuss the assignment in person – and make use of SMART attributes – and then *always* follow up the in-person discussion with an email that documents what was discussed and agreed to. (Yes, think "pixel trail".)

PART NINE

THE TIES THAT BIND
A GREAT TEAM CULTURE

CHAPTER 44

WALK & TALK, AND LUNCH WITH YOU

(If You Have a Large Team)

When you are a manager of managers, you are one step removed from the majority of your team. For example, if you have 4 managers who are your Direct Reports, and if each of them has 6 Direct Reports, then your unit has 28 people plus you – which means that you are *not* directly managing 24 people in your unit, and they don't have regular 1-to-1's with you.

If you have, say, 10 or more people with two or more Direct Report Managers reporting to you, people who report to them might feel disconnected from you.

I mention this because having layers of management beneath you makes it more challenging to create a Great Team Culture – but you can still do that if you make it a high priority to maintain a personal connection to *each person* in your unit – even if you are not managing them directly. (How do spell *m-o-r-a-l-e?*) People want to feel reassured that the big honcho "knows who I am" and "is aware of my accomplishments" and "cares about my career".

"How do I make that personal connection with so many people?" Following are two techniques that have been highly effective for me.

Walk the Hallways

Occasionally drop into people's offices (or stop by their cubicles in an open office situation)… and just say "Hello". Ask how they're doing. Ask what they're working on. But do *not* interrogate them. Do *not* start drilling down.

Do *not* ask them if they're on schedule with their project. That's the job of their manager.

Your purpose in initiating this impromptu chat is to show interest in them and in their work… without judgments. You want to get to know them – without managing them. That's it. Nothing more.

Lunch with You

Schedule *informal* lunches that are held in a conference room. This is *not* a business meeting: the gatherings should be light-hearted and fun. The purpose of this meeting is to form a deeper personal connection between you and your Directs' Direct Reports and to create greater team cohesion.

> **Note:** Frequency of the "Lunch with You" gatherings varies with how many people are on your team or in your unit. E.g., if you have 10 or fewer people, a quarterly meeting will suffice for including everyone twice a year. If, say, you have or 60 people, then you might need to meet every other month just to give everyone a chance to attend once a year – or you could hold a *monthly* "Lunch with You" so that everyone can be included twice a year. (You'll figure it out.)

In my experiences over the years, this non-business lunch meeting always goes over really well – and noticeably improves morale. Here is how to set up the *first round* of a "Lunch with You":

- Post a Lunch sign-up sheet. The first 6-10 people to sign up are "in".
- Because you want everyone to have a chance to have lunch with you, no one should attend two such lunches in a row.
- If your budget allows, order in lunch for everyone. If budget or logistics prevent you from catering the lunch, let everyone know that it's a bag-lunch affair (everyone brings their own lunch).
- Allow 1 hour if there are 8 or fewer attendees… and 1.5 hours if you have 9 or more people.
- Make photocopies of the "Self-Intro Crib Sheet" (on page 176) and hold onto them.

- When everyone has arrived, you give a low-key, 60-second introduction: e.g., "This is not a business meeting. We're here to learn a little bit more about each other – and to have fun!"
  - Now hand out a Crib Sheet to each person… and give them a minute to review it.
  - Then you say, "I'll go first"

Self-Intro Crib Sheet
(for informal lunch meetings)

1. Your name?

2. Born where?

3. Raised where?

4. Your first job?

5. Hobbies and/or leisure activities? (legal ones, only, please)

6. How long have you been at <company name>?

7. Previous job(s) in this company?

8. Previous job immediately before coming to this company?

9. Team that you are currently on? (if more than one team in your unit)

10. Current job? How long have you been doing this?

11. Briefly describe a task or project that you are currently working on.

To ensure your meeting is lively, do the following:

- *You go first.* (This is *very* important.) If you're relaxed and open-hearted and funny and honest and self-deprecating, then you've set the tone – and your team gets the message that this is indeed not a business meeting. They also get valuable clues about the type of person you are. Yes, you are the role model.
- *Jump around the table,* calling on people randomly – so no one knows when it will be their turn (except, of course, for the last person).
  - Calling on people randomly increases the chances that people will pay attention to the speaker rather than hide out and silently rehearse their comments – because they don't know when the spotlight will be turned on them.
  - Calling on people randomly also results in people turning their heads left and right, making it less likely that people will fall asleep (or get a crick in their neck).
- Alternate calling on female and male team members (to the extent possible).
- Alternate calling on senior and junior team members (to the extent possible).

The first time you host a "Lunch with You", you'll be amazed at how much good will it creates. Your team members will also be amazed because they will learn a lot about each other, which will make them a closer-knit group – which translates into improved collaboration and increased productivity. *(See the next chapter, "The Culture Gap", for additional techniques that will help you build and/or sustain a Great Team Culture.)*

Tip: If you have, say, 15 or fewer people, doing this twice a year will suffice (but do it two months in a row so that no one on your team feels deprived by having to wait many months for the opportunity).

Tip: Continue hosting "Lunch with You" meetings even after everyone in your unit has attended one such meeting. The second and future rounds become a "Q&A with the Boss", which gives everyone a chance to ask you questions about things on their minds and to hear your thinking on unit-wide and company-wide matters – and this almost always results in a lively session.

The participants can also question each other, bypassing you entirely (!), which wonderful – because it becomes a "Lunch with Teammates", which helps build and sustain a Great Team Culture.

CHAPTER 45

The Culture Gap... When You Are a Manager of Managers

The foundational tenets of the Great Team Culture you are trying to create or sustain can get "lost in translation" as the message dissipates down through the ranks. This is even more the case if your team has two levels of managers under you – which can create a "culture gap".

Even if you do a good job of inculcating your Direct Report Managers with the tenets of your team culture, and even if your Direct Report Managers do their best to pass along the team culture to their Direct Reports, a culture gap will exist to one extent or another.

Consider "Culture Fit" When Hiring a Direct Report Manager

When you are hiring a manager who will report to you, it is essential that you think a lot about whether the manager you are about to hire is a *great team fit* for the Great Team Culture you want to create or sustain.

If you have an opening for a Direct Report *Manager*, you must hire wisely. *"What does that mean in terms of team culture?"* It means that "Team Fit" must be Priority 1, so you need to ask yourself these questions:

- Will that manager-candidate understand and be capable of upholding the culture that you have put into motion and want to sustain?

- Will that manager-candidate get along with your other Direct Report Managers?

Three Techniques for Closing the Culture Gap

Here are three techniques (*aka* managerial strategies) that have worked well for me in sustaining a Great Team Culture:

- Attend a team meeting of each of your Direct Report Manager's teams twice a year.
- Hold a 30-minute skip-level 1-to-1 *twice a year* with every person in your unit. (If your team is larger than, say, 25 people, then holding a skip-level 1-to-1's *once a year* will have to suffice.)

  Note: Yes, it's a serious time commitment. Don't think for a minute that you don't have enough time to do that. You can't afford to *not* do that. Having a strong team culture – a Great Team Culture – will save you lots of time and will lead to your team's frequently exceeding expectations. Don't be lured into taking short-cuts with team-culture nourishment… because doing so will cost you dearly.

- Sponsor a non-business, casual, group-lunch meeting. *(This technique is discussed in detail in the previous chapter, ""Walk & Talk, and Lunch with You".)*

PART TEN

STRATEGY

(A FEW THOUGHTS ON)

CHAPTER 46

"THE VISION THING"

It took me a while to come around to understanding the importance of having a Vision within a large organization. I was one of those people who thought Vision statements were hot air and constantly changing – so I didn't pay much attention to company Visions. I came to learn that many people – perhaps most people in corporations – are not like me.

Many people have an emotional and intellectual need for their company to have a Vision – because it helps them see the importance of their work and understand how it fits into the greater scheme of things. That knowledge propels them to do the best work they can for customers.

For such people a company Vision is important and potent: it's the flag that they rally around. So it's wise to ensure that the company has a Vision that your team can align with. Most of your Direct Reports will want to know what the world will look like (and what their own future will look like) if the company is successful in the long term.

Let's consider an example...

Microsoft's "Vision" statement for many years was:

"a computer on every desk and in every home"

It's an interesting example of a Vision statement because:

- Microsoft did not manufacture or sell computers.
- Microsoft did not manufacture or sell desks.

- The statement contains no definitions of "success metrics" – i.e., no mention of revenue or profit margin or units sold or audience size (except for the modest mention of *"every"*).
- The statement contains no mention of budget or deadlines or features.

The Vision is an "end statement", a futuristic statement, an imagining of what the world will look like – how the world will be changed – if the long-term Vision is achieved.

Of course, Microsoft's Vision statement has been recrafted (but not often) as the high-tech world changed – with little things like mobile, cloud, game players, and software as a service cropping up. That said, the Microsoft Vision statement was indeed long-term and futuristic; it served the company very well for 25-ish years. Other companies have also had Vision statements that lasted more than a decade.

Creating a long-term Vision statement usually takes a lot of thought and innumerable iterations and sign-offs to get it right. (It is usually not as simple as "We make chocolate".) But it's worth the effort – and will repay the cost in invested time and effort many times over – because, in the process, people's ideas are clarified and tested… and improved.

Caveat: It's difficult to craft a successful Mission, Goals, or Strategy if there is no company Vision – because you won't know where things are headed long-term.

"Is this Vision Stuff Relevant to Me?"

Probably not… if you're a first-time manager or a first-line manager in a very large company. Usually high-level manager are involved in helping to shape a company's Vision. That said…

… it's good to start learning, early in your career, how higher-ups think about the business. So it's useful to have a deeper understanding of "the Vision thing".

Probably not... if you're already a high-level manager who has been part of an executive team involved in creating a Vision for a company. That said...

... I have numerous times seen senior managers struggling with definitions and working at cross-purposes because they had different conceptions of how you go about creating a Vision and perhaps were taught in different workshops by different gurus about what a Vision statement should contain – and how Mission, Goal, and Strategy statements are supposed to align with a Vision. So if your peers are not on the same page, this chapter and the following chapter might be a big help to all of you and to the company – and, ultimately, to your customers.

Caveat: If your manager and/or skip-level manager and/or company CEO have not done a Vision-creation exercise in a world-class manner, you do not want to show them up: you might embarrass them... and you do *not* want to do that. No, no, no, no, no.

"So, what should I do?" Introduce the concept to them... gently. Perhaps you say something like, *"I just read about how to create a Vision in this book I'm reading. It's an interesting model."* And then pause – to see whether their eyes light up... or glaze over.

Good luck!

CHAPTER 47

CREATING A POWERFUL VISION

I've sat through a bunch of workshops focused on Vision and Mission statements… and learned some things from each. However, none of them worked well for me, either intellectually or when put into practice. So I borrowed liberally from a number of sources and over the years pieced together and fine-tuned an approach that worked for me, for my peers, and my teams.

The table on the following page provides definitions of key characteristics of a powerful Vision in terms that I hope will work for you:

Key Characteristics of a Vision Statement *<template>*

Memorable	• Short, crisp, and easy to memorize (12 words or less). • Each person on your team or in your unit or in your company can instantly recite it.
End-state (futuristic)	• This is a long-term view: 10+ years out (no success metrics attached to the far-off future). • Describes how the world looks if the Vision becomes the reality.
Inspirational	• People are excited, energized, motivated.
Aspirational	• Strives for a lofty ambition, something greater than the present (in scope, in impact).
Compelling	• Everyone *wants* to do it, wants to see that future end-state actualized. • Everyone believes it's doable (with inspired effort and world-class execution).
Externally-facing	• The Vision is primarily customer-facing, client-facing; it's about the world outside, beyond the walls of your workplace.
Not product-specific	• The Vision does *not* mention a specific "service offering" or "product"; it can be an umbrella for multiple products and services.

No scorecard or success metrics	• No mention of revenue or profit margin. • No mention of audience size. • No mention of market share. • No mention of growth year-over-year. • No mention of location. • No mention of deadlines. • No mention of the competition. • No direct mention of the product.

CHAPTER 48

CRITERIA FOR MISSION, GOALS, STRATEGY, SUCCESS METRICS, AND TACTICS

O nce the Vision is set in stone, the next steps are to lock down on Mission, Goals, Strategies, Success Metrics, and Tactics.

I have been involved in many Vision-Mission-etc. exercises. I've seen very smart and experience managers struggle mightily to craft a Mission statement and to define Strategies and Goals – because they had read different books or attended different workshops… and there was no consensus on what the terms meant and how they aligned with each other.

To attain clarity for myself on each of these terms (and, thus, clarity for my teams), I tried to cull the best protocols and terminology that I came across – and then tweaked the definitions. Here is my version of the definitions for the following terms:

- **Mission** – What you do… your charter (which must align with the Vision).
- **Goals** – What, specifically, you need to do to achieve the Mission.
- **Strategy** – The plan(s) to achieve your Goals (and beat the competition).
- **Success Metrics** – The factors and data that are tracked to verify whether the Strategy is working and the Goal is being achieved. *(See "Success Metrics vs. Completion Metrics" in the next chapter.)*
- **Tactics** – The various things you do to actualize the Strategy in order to achieve your Goals.

Note: Often there are multiple Missions, Goals and Strategies.

Arriving at clear statements for each of these criteria is not an easy task – and it should *not* be easy. However, it is hugely important, so you need to get it right. You can't rush it. If this exercise is done in a sloppy manner – with muddled language or with generalities that are not crisp – the result will be less than optimal, and you risk perpetuating a situation of "garbage in, garbage out".

CHAPTER 49

STRATEGY

The term "Strategy" is batted around a lot, often in confusing ways... so it warrants a few comments. This brief chapter is not a deep, technical primer on Strategy creation. Rather, the intent is to provide managers who have never been involved in discussions of Strategy some sense of what a strategic framework entails.

What Is Strategy?

Strategy is about *winning*, about figuring out ways to improve one's chances of winning in the marketplace – as in, beating the competition. (That's it. Really, it's that simple... though of course it isn't simple to develop great Strategies.)

Strategies are "game plans" that you devise in order to ensure that Goals are accomplished and the Mission is fulfilled. If your Goals are wonderful, but your Strategies are not, your Goals will not be realized. And if your Strategies are wonderful, but your Tactics (implementation) are sub-par, your Strategy will not work – and your Goals will not be realized.

Understand Your Starting Point (Before Devising a New Strategy)

Strategies can and do change. Some have a brief shelf life (say, 3 months), and some have legs (say, 2 years or more). To truly understand your company's current Strategy and your unit's current Strategy, you need to go back 5 years and study the history of evolving Vision, Mission, Goals, Strategies, and Success Metrics within your company and unit. This will tell you a *lot* about your company and your unit – and will help you better understand the current Strategy.

> **Warning:** Strategies have a way of changing frequently, especially in fast-paced and highly-competitive industries. If you've only been on the job a short time, resist the urge to suggest changes in Strategy.

Sometimes what appears to be a stupid and short-sighted Strategy makes more sense if you understand the historical context and learn more about the competition. That said, the Strategy might still seem to you to be destined to fail. If you think that's the case, don't announce that in your first month on the job (unless asked). Give yourself a few months before you involve yourself in a company's strategic discussions. You don't want to be perceived as the new kid on the block being a smart-ass.

Success Metrics vs. Completion Metrics

Success Metrics can be difficult to define and difficult to measure. Success Metrics indicate whether the Strategy that is supposed to result in competitive wins is actually working.

Usually the metrics for assessing the success of a Strategy include such things as revenue, audience size, units sold or services delivered, percentage growth quarter-over-quarter, your company's growth rate versus the growth rate of your competitors, market share, and so forth. These can be valid metrics for measuring whether the company's Strategy and your team's Strategy are proving to be successful. But often these metrics are not Success Metrics: rather, they measure "what's been done" – i.e., "completion metrics" – and your company can go bankrupt while lots of stuff is getting done.

Completion Metrics merely measure whether tasks have been completed. You can complete a lot of tasks… and still lose to the competition. For example, I've frequently seen metrics based on completing a project by a certain date and coming in on budget; however, those factors are given "constraints" – *aka* Completion Metrics – but they are not Success Metrics, because they do not guarantee that your company will be successful in the marketplace. (A possible exception is that you know, in advance, the date that a competitor will release a new product or service – so to get a competitive "win", you need to launch your product or service before your competitor does.)

Success requires incisive Strategies, carefully defined Success Metrics, and flawless execution of Tactics (so that you can verify whether you're on track for competitive success).

Caveat: The road to a downward spiral is paved with "completion metrics". People can sometimes easily convince themselves that they have done a good job of defining Success Metrics – when they have not. And then they convince themselves that the Strategy is working – when it is not. And thus the ship begins to sink…

Execution *Is* Strategic

Implementation (getting it done) and execution (how efficiently it gets done) are commonly viewed as non-strategic, back-end type of activities… rather than as *strategic activities* that are critical to success. Mere implementation is not strategic. However…

… execution *is* strategic (not merely operational). If your team executes its Tactics in a world-class manner, the company's Strategy and your team's Strategy succeed. If not, the Goals are burnt toast.

Remember: World-class execution is *strategic* for every company – and for every team – which means that you need to be a driving force for *change* and for *continual improvement*. You always need to be doing things *smarter* and *faster* than your competitors do them.

CHAPTER 50

PUTTING A TOE IN STRATEGIC WATERS

New managers and first-line managers usually inherit an existing Strategy that has been devised by upper management – and their job is to lead their team in carrying out the Strategy. It's very important for new managers to understand the psycho-social and analytical history of how the Strategy came into being – by reading status reports from the past few years, which describe the Missions, Goals, and Strategies that were defined and acted upon. New managers should do their homework before entering a Strategy debate.

> **Warning:** If your manager and skip-level manager are the architects of the Strategy that you've inherited and that you think is doomed to fail, you need to tread carefully before criticizing their Strategy. At the very least, you need to find out whether they devised the Strategy or whether someone even higher up dropped the Strategy into their lap… before you rock the boat.

In the infrequent case that a new manager immediately senses that the inherited Strategy is a loser or a train wreck waiting to happen, it's important to understand that the new kid on the block is usually not listened to. It can be career-damaging to a new manager to shout out before knowing who created the strategy. However, if you're the new manager and feel strongly that the strategy needs to change – and change fast – then you'll do what you feel you need to do.

Read on before you leap…

CHAPTER 51

PREPARING TO OPEN THE "WRONG STRATEGY" CAN OF WORMS WITH YOUR MANAGER

(*Very* Carefully, of Course)

I f you feel in your gut that the Strategy you have inherited will not lead to success, you need to do the following before tentatively placing your neck on the chopping block:

- **Study the current Strategy** *deeply* to understand its strengths and weaknesses – and how and why it came to be. The strategy at some point seemed logical to a bunch of smart people, so you must begin *by understanding their train of thought and analysis* at a given point in time. To do that, begin by trying to find the answers to these questions:
  - Who in the company was involved in creation of the Strategy? (Are they still in the company? Are they still in your area or unit or division? Was it your manager or your skip-level manager?)
  - What data was the Strategy based on?
  - What were competitors doing at the time the Strategy was devised?
  - Was that data correctly interpreted?
  - Was the data accurate or specific enough?
  - Is the data still relevant and/or accurate? Or is there more recent data on which new decisions should be based?

- ○ Has the business climate changed? (New trends? Changes in cost structure and supply chain? A shrinking marketplace?)
  - ○ Were there new competitors with better strategies, lower cost structures, and/or newer technologies?
  - ○ Was the Strategy simply an example of inertia that organizations can sometimes settle into?
  - ○ Was the Strategy a desperate and quick-fire attempt to come up with something that was a game-changer because the company was losing ground to a competitor's new product or service?
  - ○ Is the Strategy outdated? (Was it a great Strategy during the years that it created a hefty cash flow, but now too much energy is going into trying to protect the cash cow rather than investing in creating new cash cows?)
  - ○ Was the Strategy a result of pressure from the board of directors or the CEO and COO and CFO? (Sometimes higher-ups are out of touch with what's happening on the ground below them.)

- **Spell out in detail** – in a draft memo to yourself – why a course-correction is needed.
- **Test your ideas** with a few people whom you trust – by getting their feedback on your draft memo – *before* discussing the current Strategy with your chain of command.
- **Calculate** the ramifications and costs of changing course – in financial, organizational, interpersonal, and customer terms (internal and external customers).
- **Think hard about possible unintended coincidences.** (Yeah, that's always difficult to do.)
- **Decide on the optimal way to raise this disturbing topic** to your manager and/or to upper management. Take into consideration the time, place, participants (who? how many?), tone, and medium for raising the topic.

Caveat: If you have been on the job for less than, say 3 months, and are 90% certain that the current Strategy is a train wreck waiting to happen, you might have to speak up soon and loudly – despite the inherent risks of doing that.

Speaking up can be a high-stakes gamble: you could end up as the scapegoat and never advance in the company or be out of a job... or you could end up the hero and be seen as a rising star.

If you're really *really* certain that the inherited strategy is doomed and that the company is in or will soon begin a downward spiral if there is no course correction, you might as well take the risk of being the new kid on the block who speaks up too soon... because if the train wreck happens, you'll be out of a job.

PART ELEVEN

ADDITIONAL THINGS THAT EVERY MANAGER NEEDS TO KNOW

CHAPTER 52

THE **OARP** MODEL –

FOR KEEPING A PROJECT ON TRACK

Keeping a project on track is not a simple thing to do, especially if there are a lot of cooks in the kitchen and if several units are involved who have different priorities. Whether the project involves a new product or service or whether it's a project in trouble that needs triaging, the OARP model can save you much time and effort – and spare you a lot of anxiety and craziness. (Full disclosure: The OARP model is not my invention.)

When managers are shepherding a project, they need to ask themselves:

- *"How do I establish a clear decision-making process?"*
- *"How do I keep the project on schedule?"*
- *"How do I avoid late-arriving design-change requests (DCRs) that key partners or upper management suddenly announce as a *must-haves*?"*
- *"How do I ensure that I will get sign-off on my product or service or feature or application from the right people?"*

Answer: I recommend that you adopt the OARP model. *(See "OARP Model – Definitions", on page 207.)*

Warning: Do *not* wait to involve the OARP role players until after you have created what you deem a "near-final" specification for the product or feature. You need their input at the front-end of the project… which is why you begin with an Alpha Spec Review. If you don't bring the role players into the loop from the get-go, you'll have to back-track – and much time will have been wasted, and your schedule will be in jeopardy early on.

"So who are the OARP players? And what do they do?" See the following table…

OARP Model – Definitions

Owner	The orchestra conductor (you!) for the project, who ensures that the various "instruments" play beautifully together – and who leads the OARP process. Manages cross-team collaboration processes. On point for the *quality* of the Project Specifications and also for the *implementation* of those Specs to deliver the project on time, on budget, and meeting or exceeding expectations.
Approver	The project sponsor, usually the manager or skip-level manager of the Owner or higher in the food chain, who must give the final go-ahead on the Final Specifications before the project can commence. (Note: It's essential that the Approver agree to or deny requests for late-breaking design-change requests.)
Reviewers	People who have specific and deep domain knowledge and who review the Specs. (They do not create the Specs; they do not do the work to create a product or feature.) If the Reviewers and the Owner disagree on some aspect of the project, then the issue is escalated to the Approver for resolution.
Participants	The people who provide input and offer comments during the shaping stages of the Project Specs. Usually involves cross-team collaboration of the people who will do the work: e.g., marketers, supply-chain planners, operational staff, graphic artists, coders, testers, writers, editors, etc. Such people perform have unique skill-sets and unique perspectives that must be incorporated into the specifications.

Note: Some people prefer the RACI model or a few similar models. I've used both OARP and RACI – and have found the OARP model to work slightly better. That said, some process is superior to no process, so choose the project-control model that you think will work best for your situation.

Alpha Spec Review

Here's how to get the OARP-model process in motion:

- Work with your manager (and perhaps your skip-level manager) to decide which people will fill the roles of Owner, Approver, Reviewers, and Participants.
- Notify the people (and their managers) that they have been selected to participate in the OARP-model review process
- Organize the first OARP meeting *well in advance*. Getting all the players into a room at the same time is difficult, so in most circumstance you need will to invite them way ahead of time.
- Create the Alpha Specification and distribute it at least 1 day ahead of the Alpha Spec Review to all the OARP players. (Some will study the spec ahead of time… and some won't. That said, the meeting will be more productive if some of the players come prepared with feedback.)
- Make copies of the Alpha Spec and pass them out at the meeting.
- Follow up the Alpha Spec Review with an email that provides a detailed summary of the meeting and the changes that will be made as a result of the feedback. Ask for comments on your detailed summary to be submitted to you within 48 hours.
- After the 48-hour limit on comments has passed, do the necessary work to refine and improve the Alpha Spec to come up with a Beta Spec.

Beta Spec Review

- Organize the Beta Spec Review meeting – inviting the OARP players. Attach the Beta Spec to your email, which should be sent at least 1 day in advance of the Beta Spec Review.

  Caveat: It's critical that the key OARP role players attend the Beta Spec Review. If they do not, then you'll almost certainly have to deal with late-breaking Design Change Requests (DCRs), which will push out your schedule and/or lead to burnout.

- Make copies of the Beta Spec and pass them out at the meeting.
- Follow up the in-person Beta Spec Review meeting with an email that provides a detailed summary of that meeting and the changes that will be made to the Beta Spec as a result of the feedback.
- After the Beta Spec has been revised, send an email to the OARP role players – and attach the updated Beta Spec. Ask for comments within 48 hours – and make clear that changes to the Spec will not be allowed after that time. (Of course, some higher-ups are likely to disobey this ultimatum, but then it will at least be clear who is responsible for the deadline having been missed.)
- Incorporate any feedback you have received on the Beta Spec, and prepare the Final Spec.
  - If some of the feedback is unclear or off-base or requiring major design changes, you need to meet with your manager immediately… and decide whether some 1-to-1 "clarification" meetings are required with the relevant players.

Final Spec Review

- Organize the Beta Spec Review – inviting the OARP players to what is hopefully the *Final* Spec Review meeting.
- Send out the Final Spec in your email at least 1 day in advance of the Final Spec Review meeting, spelling out the changes that have been made since the Beta Spec was reviewed, and making clear that all additional feedback and comments need to be submitted within 48 hours.

Note: Yes, a higher-up might overrule your request for a 48-hour turn-around, but it's important that you draw a line in the sand. If anyone wants more time, then they will have to state how much additional time they need. You must make it clear to all the OARP players that more turn-around time is likely to push out the schedule beyond the agreed-upon deadline.

Note: If the Approver and the Reviewers sign off on the Final Spec via email, then you might not need to have a Final Spec Review meeting.

- Make copies of the Final Spec and pass them out at the meeting.
- The goal of the Final Spec Review meeting is *to get sign-off* from all the necessary OARP participants – either at that meeting or within 24 hours of that meeting. Without a rock-solid Final Specification (and accompanying Ship Criteria), you and your team are in a vulnerable position.

Critical: You must *emphasize* to all the stakeholders in the OARP model that any significant changes to the Final Specs will result in *pushing out the schedule* and/or *increasing costs* – or that, to keep on schedule, some features might have to be cut and then completed after launch, or that people resources will need to be increased ASAP (of course, increasing costs), and that an additional project plan will need to be agreed on that includes an updated schedule, additional budget, and additional people resources.

If a stakeholder demands a Design Change Request at this late stage, then insist that the Approver must sign off on the DCR. That way you'll know that everyone understands the effect of the DCR on people resources, budget, and deadline. The Approver is where the buck stops.

Yes, you need to be firm… or you might get pushed around. And if they still ignore what you say, at least you have created a pixel trail (and an oral-history trail) which will later exclaim, "I told you so" – though you won't have to actually say "I told you so"… because they will be thinking that without your prompting.

Summary of Benefits of the OARP Model

Following this OARP-review protocol might seem like overkill – but it's actually the opposite: It will save you much time… and much heartache. Let me count the ways:

- It increases the odds that the project will stay within budget, meet or exceed expectations, and launch on time.
- It minimizes or prevents late-stage finger-pointing.
- It greatly reduces the chances of complaints about something having been left out or misconstrued.
- It makes clear who is responsible for omissions and mess-ups (and it usually is *not* someone on your team).
- It greatly minimizes the much-disliked and late-breaking DCRs, which are schedule killers, budget killers, resource killers, and morale killers.

Following the OARP protocol will garner respect for you and your team from the OARP role players – whether it's an urgent Triage situation or part of a non-urgent development process for a product or service or feature. Other managers and teams will learn that you and your team are professional, organized, efficient, and attentive to detail – and they will also absorb the subliminal (and not so subliminal) message that *you and your team are not to be messed with* without their running the risk of looking foolish, incompetent, and/or irresponsible.

Two Things to Remember to Do...

"Is there anything else I can do to protect my team and increase the chances of finishing the project on time and on budget?"

Yes. Do the following:

- *Analyze the schedule, the budget, and the available people resources* to be sure that they realistically align with company expectations.
- *Educate your manager* by creating a table of Benefits and Risks based on the current budget, resources, and budget.

Educating your manager will help ensure that you and your manager are on the same page – and occasionally this discussion will result in adjustments to schedule, scope, budget, and/or people resources.

Warning: The last thing you ever want your manager to say to you (if your team has missed a critical deadline) is: *"Why didn't you warn me about the risks early on when I could have done something about it? You knew how important this was. If you needed more resources to get it done, I would have made sure you had them! Or we would have cut scope."*

Ergo, educate your manager – early and often.

Best practice: Under-promise and over-deliver.

CHAPTER 53

DEVELOPING A COMMUNICATIONS STRATEGY

(Internal and External)

You don't need to create a *communications strategy* in your first week on the job. However, after a few weeks have passed, you should at least begin thinking about and outlining a communications plan... and run it by your manager for input and approval.

If, however, you've been in your current managerial role for some time and don't yet have a communications strategy, hop to!

"Why do I need a communications plan?"

For a number of reasons:

- You need to keep your colleagues informed about what you're doing, especially those colleagues with whom you don't work closely or often.
- Your peers will appreciate your communiques, particularly if you occasionally mention and praise the work that their teams are doing.
- The communiques that you author make it easy for your manager to keep your skip-level manager up-to-speed on what your team is accomplishing... and your skip-level manager can then inform her/ his peers as well as those higher in the command chain.
- Your own team will be happy that they are getting exposure for the work they do, and will view your communiques as a sign that you're a Great Manager.

Identify Your Potential Audiences

Think about the people or teams that you need to keep informed – and get your manager's sign-off. Here are some that come to mind:

- Your team
- Your peers
- Your manager
- Your manager's peers
- Your skip-level manager
- Your skip-level manager's peers
- The division Vice President (or perhaps your manager or skip-level manager will inform the division V.P.)
- The CEO (or perhaps your division VP will inform the CEO)
- Your internal customers (in other units, other divisions, with whom you don't have a close working relationship)
- Your external customers (who buy your products or services)

How Often Should Each Audience Receive a Status Report from You?

The optimal frequency of status reports can change over time and can vary with audience – and you will need to craft different status reports for different audiences. For example, if you are reporting on a long-term project that will take 6 months to deliver/launch, then a monthly status report is probably OK for the first 2 months – and then switch to biweekly status reports for next 2 months, and then to weekly status reports for the next 6 weeks. As the pace picks up during the last 2 weeks of the project, daily status reports are usually a good idea for those who are involved in the daily production/creation work.

Best Practice: Generally, the people closest to you and your team should receive frequent status reports... and those people or teams who are more remote from you should receive status reports less often.

Frequency of issuing status reports also depends on company culture, on the desires of your manager and skip-level manager, and on the desires of the recipients of the status reports. Be sure that you discuss your communication plans with your manager, who might have strong views on this topic.

What Format Should You Use for Status Reports?

It's possible that your manager or skip-level manager or division head has a standardized Status Report form. If no such form exists, create a draft form and get some feedback from a few experienced people you trust. After tweaking, run it by your manager for approval.

> **Best Practice:** You will save yourself a lot of time and effort if you develop a *modular format* for status reports that allows you to create a "Master Status Report" from which you can easily pull out (or shorten) modules of content for shorter status reports as needed for your different audiences. That way you reuse content and minimize "reinvention of content" – and you avoid having to deal with multiple formats that differ significantly from each another and therefore require lots of tweaking.

CHAPTER 54

Which Member of Your Team Will Come Up with the Next Break-Through Idea?

The answer is: *You can't know.* You cannot see into the future.

The next Great Idea could come from that aggressive-in-meetings person who talks a lot and comes up with five ideas per meeting. It could come from that shy person who rarely says a word at team meetings (which you should not allow to continue). It could come from the person who has only one original idea each year. Or it could come from the seemingly most-brilliant or least-brilliant person on your team.

> **Moral of the story:** You cannot predict which of your Direct Reports will come up with the next break-through idea. No fool-proof data points are available to help you make such predictions – and past experience won't help in this case.

"So what am I supposed to do with that reality?

You create a Great Team Culture that does not constrain creative thinking. You create a Great Team Culture that invites and expects contributions from everyone… at any time.

"How do I do that?"

For starters read (or reread) the chapters on *"How to Run Effective Team Meetings"* and on *"The Art of 1-to-1 Meetings with Your Direct Reports"*. Put them into practice – and you'll be on your way to encouraging and harvesting the best out-of-the-box thinking.

Remember: Creating a Great Team Culture is a *key strategy* in developing an innovative and high-performance team.

CHAPTER 55

"MANAGING" YOUR PEERS... EFFECTIVELY

Progress in large organizations often requires cross-team collaboration, so building productive relationships with your peers is crucial. Success in this arena is relatively easy – if you do the following:

- Meet with each of your peers 1-to-1 over lunch – once a month or, if that isn't possible due to everyone's busy schedules, at least once a quarter.
  - There's something about food, about sharing a meal, that is calming and makes the meeting more human and less business-like.
  - Having lunch out also means that you're not going to be interrupted by a Direct Report walking into either of your offices or an office landline phone ringing.
  - Later, after you've met a few times over lunch and know each other, and if you have an urgent or semi-urgent situation, you can go into high gear immediately and skip the social pleasantries.
- Ask your peers what your team can do better.
- Ask your peers whether there is anything that your team could do to help their team succeed.
- Make clear to your peers how important they and their team are to you and your team (without sounding wimpy or unctuous).
- When you run into the Direct Reports of your peers, let them know how much you appreciate them.

- Invite your peers to one of your team meetings, and ask them to do a presentation about their team's projects. (I've never had a peer turn down that request/offer.)
    - This invitation almost always results in reciprocity – an offer you'll gladly accept when it arrives.
- When you have an opportunity to speak at an "All Hands" meeting, where your team and your peers' teams attend a large meeting with your manager-in-common or skip-level manager-in-common, be sure to mention the efforts of other teams that contributed to your team's success – or resentment and hurt feelings will be the result.

    Caveat: This can be dicey if you bestow accolades on one or a few teams or people but not on the others who are present. Think through potential unintended consequences so that you can be confident that you won't be insulting any peer or any team or person whom you do not mention.

    Note: An important side-benefit of helping to build greater cooperation and cohesion among your peers is that your manager and skip-level manager will usually notice that you're a team player who enhances collegiality.

If your peers don't respond positively to your outreach, wait a while... and then try again a month later (perhaps taking a different tack). They might have hesitated because:

- They don't know whether you're trustworthy.
- They might think that you're a touchy-feely type... and they're not comfortable with that.
- They don't know what your charter is (does it conflict with theirs?) or they fear that your charter and their charter overlap, which makes them tense.
- They might fear that you're angling to absorb their team into yours... and that you're using the 1-to-1's with them to learn more about their business for "expansionist" reasons.

- They might be very busy or in crisis mode, and your outreach to them at a certain point in time is a Priority 3.

The first few 1-to-1's with your peers are likely to be a feeling-out process (unless you already know them and/or have worked with them). Your peers might be a little cautious at first and might do some subtle or not-so-subtle prodding to try to get a measure of you and what charter you've been given. So expect that initial dance – and be patient with your peers. Think like a farmer: plow the soil, plant seeds, fertilize, harvest... and repeat.

If you think about relationship-building as a long-term play rather than as a short-term gambit, the chances are good that you will succeed in building excellent working relationships with your peers.

Tip: When one of your peers moves on, move quickly to establish a good working relationship with the new peer.

Best Practice: You *always* have time to meet with your peers if they request a meeting with you – no matter how busy you are. Never say, "No, I can't. I'm busy this week." If you want them to be there for you in a time of need, then you need to be there for them in a time of need.

If you really can't meet with them at the time that they suggest, be sure to immediately offer two or three alternative times that would work for you. (Maybe an early breakfast before the workday starts... or a post-work meet-up away from the office.)

Remember: Great relationships with your peers can sometimes be essential to your success. If you've studied Power Lab theory or been to Power Lab training, you will know that when peers band together, they have a much better chance of influencing upper management than if they try to convince upper management flying solo.

CHAPTER 56

WHAT IF SOMEONE MAKES YOU ANGRY?

(Be *Very* Careful)

We've all had the experience of feeling tension in our lungs and a thumping heartbeat when someone says something at a meeting or writes an email that is insulting or critical of you or your team. We might feel an overwhelming urge to get back at that person. Call it self-defense. Call it revenge. Or think of it as the "fight" in the "fight or flight" corner of our ancient brains. We are tense and angry... and feel threatened.

When you feel this way, be very aware that you have entered THE DANGER ZONE. You need to resist the urge to do or say or write something impulsively that you will regret later. (I've made that mistake – and learned the hard way *not* to do it.)

At such moments you need time to be thoughtful – and to exhibit *grace under duress.* Yes, easier said than done... but doable. Here are some tips for extricating yourself from The Danger Zone:

- At first, do nothing.
- "Stay calm, have courage, and wait for signs." These words are spoken by Standing Bear, a Cheyenne who is a lifelong friend of Sheriff Longmire in *"As the Crow Flies"*, a novel in Craig Johnson's wonderful Sheriff Longmire mystery series that takes place in Wyoming. (Mr. Johnson informed me that this saying is the sign-off from a Cree Radio Station in Canada.) It's good advice, both at work and in your non-work life.

Caveat: Try to avoid replying in email when a person has made you angry. Email is a terrible medium for emotion because what you write can instantly be forwarded to many people… and there is no way to retract your words.

If a face-to-face meeting is not possible, and your only recourse is to deal with the matter in email, follow this protocol to minimize the chances of your email having terrible consequences:

1. Open a new email.
2. Put your own email address on the To: line. (Yes, you're sending this to yourself.)
3. Put "DRAFT" on the Subject: line, and then…
4. Write the most hard-hitting, angry, and sarcastic response that you are capable of writing, putting all your venom into the DRAFT email text.
5. Send the email to yourself… but do *not* read the email for at least 4 hours – and preferably wait until the next day to re-read your angry DRAFT again.
6. Now that you're calm*ing* down (I won't yet say "calm*ed* down"), think again about whether to respond and how you want to respond.
7. If you decide that you are going to respond in email, write a new *non-angry* "NEW DRAFT", using your best professional smarts and mature professional tone.
8. Show this "NEW DRAFT" to one or two people whose judgment you trust, and get their feedback. (These trusted advisors should be psychologically sophisticated *and also* have good business sense.)
9. Roll in the feedback… and write a FINAL DRAFT.
10. Create a fresh email, with an appropriate (non-incendiary) title on the Subject line, and copy and paste in your final text… and before you click "Send", double-check that you're sending the correct draft.

You'll feel much better. You'll feel much wiser.

CHAPTER 57

WHAT IS THE ONE GUARANTEED MOTIVATOR?

D id you guess *"money"*? Nope. Guess again…

Job security? Nope. In very bad economic times – e.g., during the Great Depression early in the 20th century in the United States – job security was a motivator of sorts… though having a job was akin to the removal of a de-motivator. In good economic times, job security is not something folks are anxious about, so it doesn't motivate them. (If the economic times are really good, some people are always looking for their next opportunity and don't worry at all about job security.)

Having a good manager? That can help, but not always… or not always enough.

Getting visibility from higher-ups in the company? For some, that can be a motivating factor… but it tends to be a short-lived motivation. And some folks don't give a hoot about what higher-ups think.

The answer is… **Success.**

People are motivated by their own success. If people feel successful, they become *self-motivated*. Being successful energizes them… and often makes them hungry for new challenges and stretch assignments.

Research galore on motivation has been done over the decades, and the motivating factors can shift with changes in culture, location, economic climate, and other variables. However, the one factor that has shown up repeatedly over the decades as a reliable motivator – usually as the most reliable motivator – is *people's own success*.

It's easy to understand why this is true. Lots of good things can happen when a person feels successful. For example, the person:

- Feels good.
- Is admired by others.
- Gets kudos from their manager (and hopefully also from their skip-level manager, which you can help make happen).
- Imagines good things happening in the future, such as:
    - Might get a mention at unit meetings or divisional meetings or in an internal communique.
    - Might be given a more interesting or challenging assignment.
    - Might get a promotion.

If your Direct Reports are successful, you don't have to keep coming up with all kinds of gimmicks and techniques to motivate them…. because your Direct Reports will become *self-motivated*. (Of course, there's nothing wrong with some motivational tricks and individual recognition.)

Best Practice: The most effective way to motivate your Direct Reports is to *create conditions that increase their chances of success* at whatever they're working on. If you do this – and this is your key responsibility – you have optimized the chances of your Direct Reports experiencing success… and the result will be that each member of your team will be self-motivated.

If your Direct Reports are self-motivated, the chain of command will view you as a Great Manager… which, of course, you are.

CHAPTER 58

THE DIFFICULT DANCE OF OPPOSING PRINCIPLES

A ll of us are sometimes caught in a situation where two of our ideals or two of our ideas are in conflict. You will make the best decisions when you allow the opposing thoughts to speak to you. Two principals that can and should collide in the workplace are:

- Believe what you think with your whole heart.
- Don't believe everything you think.

Colliding Principal #1:
Believe What You Think with Your Whole Heart

"Why is this important?" Because, as a manager, you live in a glass jar – and everyone is watching you all the time. You have to be constantly aware that your mood is infectious, which can be either good or bad, depending on what you're feeling. Never underestimate this reality.

If you're confident and relaxed, those around you will likely be confident and relaxed – and your team will exhibit a can-do attitude. If you are anxious, somber, nasty, argumentative, or depressed, your team will notice or sense that. They might even absorb some of your less-attractive moods – and the can-do attitude will shift toward negativity.

Note: You do not have to be fake-smiley all the time: you simply need to be keenly aware of how powerfully your mood and behavior affect your team and other teams around you.

Yes, you are the role model – actually, much more than your team's role model. You are the most constant presence in their work-lives. If you are not whole-heartedly convinced that what your team is doing is the right thing, they will not buy into the Great Team Culture that you are striving to create. Your behavior and words must communicate that the team is on the road to success (or not).

I am *not* suggesting that you fake it. Au contraire, I'm saying that if you're heart isn't in it, you need to course-correct – for your good, for the good of your team, and for the good of the company.

Colliding Principal #2:
Don't Believe Everything You Think

"Why is this important?" Because sometimes what we think is true is *not* true. We might be wrong or be missing the boat on some issue. Sometimes your strategy will not be working – and everyone on your team knows it – except you. That is a terrible position for you to be in.

You don't want to know *less* about what is not working than your Direct Reports know or your manager and your skip-level manager know. Such absence of self-awareness and myopia about what is happening around you can be enough to force your manager to show you the door or make you a sole contributor.

Usually you will have some sense that things are not working out the way you planned… and, if so, you need to ask yourself: *"What if I'm wrong?"* Your body will usually give you early-warning signals about the error of your ways (before your brain has figured it out). Trust your gut: if you're anxious or nervous, your physical being already knows something that your intellectual being hasn't figured out yet.

Here are some early-warning signals that you might be wrong. You should pay a lot of attention if:

- You notice that you're feeling more anxious than before... and you don't know why.
- You start dreading 1-to-1's with your manager.
- You start working longer hours, and this snuck up on you... and you don't know why.
- You shoot off an email impulsively and realize the moment that you hit "Send" that you should not have sent that email... and you wonder how you could have been so stupid – and wonder why you sent it.
- You're tense because more than one of your Direct Reports has asked for permission to interview elsewhere – or you learn from the grapevine that a couple of your Direct are quietly job-hunting – and you're not sure why they are looking around for other opportunities.
- You're avoiding eye contact with your Directs – and you don't know why.
- Your Directs are avoiding eye contact with you – and you don't know why.
- You suddenly start looking at data and success metrics, trying to figure out why they are wrong or misleading.
- You're tense when you get home from work, and you're tense all evening.
- You have trouble falling asleep.
- You don't sleep well, waking numerous times during the night, and you wake up in the morning tired instead of refreshed.
- You're tense in the morning before you leave home and head to the office.
- You start getting edgy Sunday afternoon, ending the weekend early.

Note: These early-warning signals tell you that something is not right in your universe – but you can't address them until you take the crucial first step of questioning your thoughts and beliefs. Yes, this is difficult – but it isn't as difficult as having the situation blow up around you – and then having to go into emergency gear to try to figure out how to fix it.

Caveat: You can experience these early-warning signals for reasons having nothing to do with being wrong. You might be worried about some company rumor you heard... or sensing that your manager has been tense with you of late, and you don't know what that's about. Or perhaps you're tense because of issues happening on the home front. So it is important to be aware of these signals – and then try to figure out, ASAP, which circumstances are causing the symptoms.

Warning: You probably noticed that the early-warning signals are almost all bodily signals. If you live entirely in your head, you'll get in trouble... fast. The old maxim has it right: *trust your gut.* Your instincts, your gut, are usually more accurate than your mental machinations. Your intellect can play all kinds of games with your mind. Your body doesn't lie. *Trust your gut, trust your gut, trust your gut.*

Best Practice: It's healthy and wise to make a habit of questioning your beliefs. If you never do that, you'll be missing out on some great learning.

A great mental-gymnastics exercise is to assume that you are wrong 50% of the time, and then ask yourself: *"What would I do differently if I thought that my thinking or solution was wrong?"* Great insight often emerges from such meditations.

Best Practice: To help keep alert and open-minded and humble, repeat these statements to yourself once a day (or at least once a week):

- *"I am allowed to make mistakes."*
- *"I am allowed to make course-corrections; they are critical to business success."*
- *"My Direct Reports are sometimes smarter and wiser than I am."*
- *"My Direct Reports sometimes have a more objective view of a situation."*
- *"My only irreversible mistake is a mistake that I don't recognize or that I resist fixing."*

If you have created a Great Team Culture in which honest and open exchange of ideas is encouraged, you'll be sitting pretty because the early-warning system will have become a *team responsibility.*

59

There's Never Enough Time to Do It Right... But There's Always Enough Time to Fix It

O ne of the most profound learnings I absorbed in my twenties was from one of my mentors. When Lilian Malt *(see "Remembrances" at the end of this book)* and I co-conducted week-long manager-training seminars, one of the most-often heard complaints was that things went wrong because *there wasn't enough time or budget or resources to get it right.* In the first seminar that I co-led with Lillian, this issue was raised – and everyone jumped in with the same complaint. Lillian (30 years my senior) calmly asked: *"So what did you do?"*

The answer always was: *"We had to fix it."*

Lillian then calmly asked: *"How much time did it take you to get it right?"*

The answer always was some form of: *"A lot of time. Too much time."* (Often the fix required 25-75% more time than initially allotted for the project!!!)

Lillian then calmly asked: *"How much did the fix cost you?"*

The answer always was some form of: *"A lot. It put us way over the original budget."* (Often the fix was 25-75% over the original budget for the project!!!)

Lillian would sigh, roll her eyes slowly (but not too dramatically), sigh, do an almost indiscernible shake of her head, and then muse: *"Isn't it funny that there's never enough time or budget or people power to get it right the first time, but there's always enough time and budget to fix it?"* (Yes, a moment of high drama!) And then she would pause, look around the table with an amused and inquiring look, and say, "It's time for our morning break"... knowing that there was lots of pent-up emotion about this topic – and that this topic would be the buzz among the managers during their break.

And that's precisely what Lillian wanted: to let the managers commiserate, and allow time for the reality to sink in that their dilemma is not unique, that the never-enough-time syndrome is a common occurrence.

When the break was over, a heated and heartfelt discussion invariably followed, with much frustration and venting, that went on for a long time – easily for 2 hours – and usually the outcries were similar, regardless of where in the U.S. the seminar was held, regardless of which industries the managers came from, and regardless of whether the managers were executives or middle managers or front-line managers.

Do any of these comments resonate with you?

- *"My boss handed me the timeline and budget... and I didn't have any say in it."*
- *"My boss said, 'Get it done on time... or I'll find someone who can.'"*
- *"The specs from <name the department> were always changing, so we had to keep redoing our work and updating the specs... and that put us behind schedule and over budget."*
- *"We'd been working on a product launch for 4 months, and a couple of days before the launch some new demands came out of nowhere – from on-high – and it destroyed our schedule and broke our budget."*
- *"We heard that our main competitor was about to launch a new product (or feature) similar to ours, and we had to get to market before they did in order to preserve or gain market share."*
- *"I didn't have all the needed skill-sets on my team to deliver the project on time, on budget, and meeting the quality bar; and I had no vendor budget, and no other department would loan me the needed talent to complete the project."*

- *"Upper management didn't have a clue of what was involved. They didn't understand that a very complicated project could not be completed in the timeframe they shoved down our throats. What am I supposed to do when upper management has totally unrealistic expectations?"*

I heard statements like these in every manager-training workshop that I facilitated as an external consultant. The outcries that I heard from all sorts of managers are grounded in complex realities – and they create very difficult circumstances for managers. (That's why they pay you the big bucks.)

"Is there anything that I can do to minimize how often or how severely this get-it-out-the-door pressure affects me and my team?"

Yes, there are a few techniques that you should try... and they are presented earlier in this book. Understand: they are not guaranteed to always work. That said, they sometimes *do* help to one degree or another... so it's worth a try. Go back and take a look at:

- Part Four: *"Triaging Your Way Out of a Mess" (Chapters 14-17)*
- Chapter 52: *"The OARP Model – for Keeping a Project on Track"*

CHAPTER 60

PERFECTIONITIS

(a Good Way to Lose Market Share)

"*Perfection is the enemy of the Good.*" (I didn't coin this phrase; it's been around a long time.)

- Perfection can also be the enemy of the Very Good.
- Perfection is seldom (if ever) achieved. If perfection is your end-goal, then your release/launch time-line will get stretched out... and you might end up launching your service or product too late – as in, after your competitors have launched a competitive product or service that is better than your existing product or service.

You can do these things to prevent Perfectionitis from getting a grip on you:

- Set reasonable, achievable, and competitor-beating criteria for launching a service or product. Then...
- Launch the product or service... and hawk early customer feedback. Then...
- Fix low-hanging-fruit problems. Then...
- Re-launch. Then...
- Innovate... and launch the new or improved product or service.

In other words, do *not* wait for perfection: launch the product or service... and keep moving forward. Resist the obsessive-compulsive urge to achieve perfection. It will kill your schedule. It will kill your budget. And it runs the risk of burning out your team.

Exception: If the product could harm people if not designed and manufactured perfectly, then you must work toward perfection and might have to adhere to tough regulations.

I'm *not* advocating that your team or your company ship a crappy product or service. I *am* saying that there is "good enough" – meaning *"very good"* – which is sufficient to please customers and bring in revenue to keep your company afloat and to grab market share.

Market circumstances are always changing. Ideas about new features are always bubbling up. So launch your product or service when it's "good enough" – and then get to work on the even-better next version. Waiting for perfection is illusory because no product or feature or service is ever perfect in everyone's eyes: e.g., team members and customers can differ as to which features are most important and which are or are not perfectly rendered.

Caveat: If you find yourself succumbing to perfectionist tendencies, you need to have a heart-to-heart with your manager about what's "good-enough" and what's "very good".

The decision about what's good-enough to ship should not rest solely on your shoulders. There should be detailed Launch Criteria that have been signed off on by upper management and that you are signed up to follow.

Warning: If Launch Criteria do not exist – and that's a *very serious danger signal* – you need to define what those launch criteria are and what a realistic schedule is, get your manager's sign-off… and then get off the perfectionist treadmill before you and your team crash and burn.

CHAPTER 61

LUTAS AND OTHER TIPS
FOR EXEC REVIEWS

Some years ago I was deposed in a contract dispute regarding an ergonomic invention of mine that was patented. In prepping me for the deposition, my attorney (David Binney) said "Remember LUTAS." Of course, I gave him a blank look… and he chuckled.

LUTAS is an acronym (devised by Binney) that incorporates useful advice for a witness to follow when the witness in a court proceeding and is being cross-examined. Hopefully, you will never be involved in a lawsuit. However, as a manager, you are very likely to be grilled by higher-ups at Executive Reviews.

Some managers think that they can show the executives how smart they are by answering their questions quickly and confidently. Some managers are shy and hesitant – and do not want to make a mistake, and perhaps do not say enough. Some managers experience "stage fright" at an Executive Review – and freeze up. Some managers have difficulty focusing. Some managers have a tendency to babble on and on – and their response goes beyond the scope of the question.

You will benefit from memorizing the LUTAS acronym and what each letter represents – and putting it to good use. Here's what LUTAS stands for:

L	**Listen** and *focus intently* on the questioner (as in, eye contact). Do not begin to answer until the executive has finished speaking – because that will get you into trouble.
U	**Understand** *before* you respond. If you don't understand the question, then say so by using expressions such as: *"Are you asking me (x), or are you asking me (y)?"* Or: *"Could you reword that so I can be sure I understand what information you're looking for?"*
T	**Think** *before* you answer. (Sounds obvious, but I've seen many managers immediately start talking out of nervousness... and then they ramble on.)
A	**Answer** *only* the question you are asked. (I have seen many managers go off the deep end because they segue into other topics and then get nailed to the wall.) After you have answered *only* the question you are asked, then you...
S	**Shut up.** Yeah, as in *stop talking.* (If you're at all nervous, you might start rambling and raise topics that will land you in deep doo-doo or lead you away from the presentation that you spent so much time and effort carefully preparing. If the Executives desire more information or some clarification, they will ask.)

The 2/3 Rule for Presentations

It is often the case that a manager is promised a certain amount of time for a presentation – whether for a slide-deck or oral-only presentation, but circumstances can cause the 30-minute presentation to shrink to 20 minutes or the 60-minute presentation shrink to 40 minutes.

"Why does that often happen?" Here are a few of the reasons:

- The meeting starts late, so you will have your time on stage shortened.
- A last-minute item or two are added to the meeting agenda, so the other agenda items have to donate some minutes to make time for the late-breaking items.
- If you are late in the line-up of speakers, your time to present will often be curtailed because the earlier presentations ran longer than

scheduled. (That might be the presenter's fault… or it might be due to the executives asking a lot of questions of an earlier speaker.)

- Equipment problems sometimes occur (e.g., with the microphone, the slide projector).
- An executive's cellphone beeps – and the exec leaves the room for some unknown emergency, saying only: *"My apologies. I'll be back in 10 minutes."*
- An executive announces that they have to catch an airplane, so the meeting will need to end 15 minutes before the scheduled ending time.

Agenda time-allotments can be altered in mid-meeting. There isn't much you can do about it – except to *prepare mentally*. That preparation is the "2/3 Rule", which tells you that if are given 30 minutes for your presentation, be prepared to tell your story in 20 minutes. And if you are given 60 minutes for your presentation, be prepared to tell your story in 40 minutes. That requires thinking in advance about which parts of your presentation you skip or shorten – and still get your main points across.

The 3-Minute Rule for Presentations

If you'll be using a slide deck for your presentation, plan on each slide that you present taking an average of 3 minutes. The complexity of a slide will determine how much time you need for that slide. However, if you think that it will only take you 30-60 seconds to present each of your slides, or perhaps even 2 minutes, you might be wondering why I recommend a "3-minute rule". Here's why:

- When people rehearse, they often practice their oral presentation "in their mind". However, when the presentation is given aloud – with pauses and changes in cadence (for dramatic emphasis) – it always takes more time than when rehearsed.
- Your audience will interrupt you with questions or comments – and you will need to respond. That takes up time – sometimes a lot of time.

The 3-minute rule means that if you are given 15 minutes for your presentation, you need to plan to tell your story in 5 slides or less... and if you are given 60 minutes for a presentation, you need to plan to tell your story in 20 slides or less.

How to Structure Your Slide-Deck Presentation

Because you can't know for sure how much time you will actually have to do your presentation, you need to think proactively about which slides you could skip or touch on only very briefly and still be able to present your core themes.

You should prepare *two* presentation decks:

- A *full-length* slide deck – which you can use if you will have the amount of time you were promised.
- A *2/3-length* slide deck – in case you learn on the spot that your time allotment has been severely shortened. (It shouldn't take you very long to create this slide deck if you have structured your deck in a modular way: you simply eliminate the less-critical slides that are not needed to tell your core story.)

Tip: Place the slides that you eliminate from your full deck (to create a 2/3-length deck) into an Appendix. You can easily access them if the executives ask questions or request more information than is contained in your 2/3-length slide deck.

CHAPTER 62

EMAIL NO-NO'S

Improper use of email is a most-excellent way to destroy a Great Team Culture. I'm not merely talking about "email etiquette" (as in, watch your language). I'm talking about something more serious and more damaging.

The two types of *never-send* emails are:

- *Never* send emails to your Direct Reports in the evening, after work hours.
  - This sends the not-so-subtle message to your Directs that you expect them to be on email and working in the evening.
  - That might not be your intent, but you are the boss… and everyone wants to please the boss. So what you're doing is modeling bad behavior – and your team will be heading toward burn-out and resentment. (Yes, they might email you in the evening, and you can decide whether you want to answer them in the evening.)
- *Never* send emails to your Direct Reports over the weekend.
  - This sends the not-so-subtle message to your Directs that you expect them to be alert for work-related email all-day Saturday, and all-day Sunday.
  - Again, that might not be your intent, but you are the boss… and everyone wants to please the boss. So what you would be doing is modeling bad behavior.

Warning: Ignore these two bits of advice, and you will undermine the Great Team Culture that you're trying to create.

Exceptions: Yes, there are always exceptions to "never" – though you should try to ensure that those exceptions are rare. If there is an *emergency*, then you and your Direct Reports must deal with it ASAP.

If your business is open on Saturday and/or Sunday, then ignore this warning. (But if you're business is closed on, say, Monday and/or Tuesday, then do not send emails on those days.)

If you are managing a team that has customers or colleagues in multiple time zones, you might have to send emails late at night or early in the morning. (E.g., when I managed a worldwide business, I would get up at 5:00am to respond to urgent emails from Europe or Africa before those folks closed down for the day.)

Similarly, I would sometimes send emails in the evening – from home, after dinner – to Asian countries and to Australia and New Zealand. In both cases, I did not want an issue to linger for 2 business days.

But – and this is *very important* – I did not Cc: any of my Directs at those very-off-hours emails: I waited until I got to the office and then, in my team's time zone, I forwarded the emails to those Directs who needed to be in-the-know. (Yeah, they might see the time-stamps (which I sometimes deleted) – and they appreciated that they weren't bombarded with emails from the moment they woke up in the morning or just before going to sleep at night.)

"What if my Direct Reports are working in a worldwide business, and they are the ones who need to send emails or make telephone calls in off-hours?"

You need to discuss this with your Directs – and come up with a policy that everyone thinks is fair. For example, your team might decide that if a person has to have a conference call between 8:00pm and 5:00am with customers or colleagues in far-off lands, the Direct gets comp time – say, 1 hour of a conf call or email creation during off-hours = 2 hours of credit – so the Direct gets to work a shorter day in the coming week (and catch up on sleep).

The critical thing is that your Directs do not burn out, that they feel that you have their health top-of-mind, and that you are aware of and appreciate that they are going the extra mile to please customers worldwide and/or support distant colleagues.

Remember: If your Direct Reports feel that you are concerned about their health and their non-work-life, then you have further stoked the Great Team Culture fires!

CHAPTER 63

"*Isn't It Enough to Be Fair?*"

Every manager at some point finds her/himself in a situation where a Direct Report is unhappy with something you said or did. You think it's a bum rap because you made serious attempts to treat that Direct fairly – and you always try to treat all your Directs fairly. At such times, it's natural to feel unfairly attacked… and you're also thinking that *"Being fair should suffice"*.

Well, it is not enough to be fair: you must be *perceived* as fair. If you *are* being fair, but some members of your team think you are *not* being fair, you've got a problem.

The reality is: Your Direct Reports cannot know how your mind works and cannot know how hard you've tried to treat people on your team in a fair way. So how can they know that you are in fact being fair?

You need to do two things to be *perceived as fair*:

- Be transparent about the decisions that you make (e.g., about work assignments).
  - You need to do this *more than once* for each significant decision – because people forget.
  - Putting decisions in writing can help greatly – because people sometimes misconstrue what you've said and sometimes space out (egads!) in team meetings and don't hear what you've said.
- A new team member will not have heard an explanation that you made at a team meeting or in an email before they joined the team;

so whenever a new person joins your team, it's a great opportunity to reiterate an explanation when you bring the new person up-to-speed. Tell your team both *how* and *why* you make decisions.

- ○ It's far better to do this proactively… before you've made a decision – and before mistrust and confusion are given an opportunity to fester.
- ○ The *"why"* is very important. You might think that everyone will automatically understand your *"why"* because you were transparent about the *"how"* – but that is not always the case. You need to get in a habit of saying, *"This is what I considered before making the decision, and this is why I made that decision."*

Best Practice: If you integrate "being perceived as fair" as a part of your management style, you will have very few (if any) complaints about fairness. That doesn't mean that all your Directs will always agree with or like each of the decisions you've made, but at least there won't be any paranoia about hidden agendas or favoritism.

A belief that a manager has "favorites" on a team is not uncommon. Favoritism – real or imagined – undermines the creation and maintenance of a Great Team Culture. Here are questions to ask yourself to help you understand the ways in which your Direct Reports might think that you have "favorites" on the team.

- Are any of your Direct Reports your personal friends (i.e., outside of work)?
- Were any of your Directs previously your peers?
- Did you have a prior work relationship with any of your Directs (say, on another team in the company or in another company)?
- Did you go to the same university as any of your Directs?
- How do you make decisions about whom you give stretch projects?
- Do you give everyone stretch goals and stretch projects?
- Are you dating anyone on your team?
- Are any of your Direct Reports dating each other?
- Do you socialize outside of work any of your Direct Reports?

As you answer these questions, you might discover some red flags that you need to think about carefully – and perhaps take corrective action – to ensure that everyone perceives you as fair.

Remember: Perception is reality. Perception is reality. Perception is reality.

CHAPTER 64

DELIVERING BAD NEWS

Delivering bad news is never easy, never fun. That said, there are better and worse ways to do it. Here are some guidelines to help you deliver bad news in the least harmful manner.

Best Practice: Be sure that you communicate unpleasant or painful decisions in the same way that you communicate pleasant and easy decisions.

Worst Practice: Delivering good news in person and bad news in email is cowardly. Deliver both good and bad news face-to-face whenever possible. (Yes, sometimes, in large organizations, especially if the team works in multiple locations, face-to-face announcements are not possible. Possible workarounds are conference calls, individual telephone calls, a videotaped "speech", or a live broadcast of a meeting.)

Best Practice: Don't allow your office to become only the bad-news place. Make sure that it's also the good-news place... or your directs will shudder every time you ask them to come to your office.

Best Practice: Always deliver bad news to individuals or to your entire team *in person*. Do *not* hide behind an email or a hard-copy memo that you place in their mailboxes or slip under their door or place on their desk.

Best Practice: After you communicate the bad news face-to-face, be sure to follow up with an email explaining the bad news, both to document the bad news and to help ensure that your words were heard accurately.

Warning: Never deliver bad news via email during the last few of hours of the day. It isn't fair. People are then heading home with a sinking feeling in their stomach because they haven't had a chance to ask questions of you or discuss the situation with their teammates.

Best Practice: Deliver bad news *in the early morning*, so a single Direct Report or your entire team has a chance to drop by your office and talk some more. Yeah, that means you have to face the person or the team all day long after you deliver bad news, and one or more of them are not feeling great and not particularly fond of you at that moment. That's part of being a Great Manager... putting the team's needs before your own.

Warning: Never, never, *never* deliver bad news on a Friday. If it has to be on a Friday, do it early in the morning. Delivering bad news on a Friday afternoon is abusive... because you've ruined your Direct Reports' Friday evening *and* their entire weekend. (I have seen more than a few managers deliver bad news on a Friday afternoon... and then slip out of the office to avoid reactions.)

Always ensure that there is time for your Directs to process the news and to ask questions. There will often be delayed reactions, so questions and concerns will arise in the minds of your Directs some hours (or even days) after you delivered the news.

Be Aware: Even if the bad news is only for one of your Directs, others on your team will likely hear about it. So if you handle the situation poorly, your entire team will know within a day or two. If you handle the situation in a world-class manner, your entire team will know that, too.

CHAPTER 65

WHAT IS THE MOST IMPORTANT THING YOU DO AS A MANAGER?

This is a no-brainer, right?

Create conditions that allow others to succeed

Yes, I keep mentioning this… because it is crucial to your team's success and to your success. *(See Chapter 2, "Good Manager vs Great Manager – the Differentiators".)*

PART TWELVE

MAINTAINING YOUR SANITY

CHAPTER 66

WORRY-FREE VACATIONS

(or Are You Constantly on Edge?)

Decades ago someone did a survey about why U.S. executives tended to not take vacations – or only took very short ones. (This survey was done in the days before global and instant email or smartphone communication.) It turned out that in most cases they were scared that if they went away for 2-5 weeks and everything ran just fine, their boss would think they were not really needed... and they would get fired. A sad state of affairs...

The truth is the opposite: one of the proof-points that a manager is a Great Manager (rather than merely a Good Manager or a So-So Manager) is that the Great Manager can take a long, worry-free vacation and everything works just fine... because that Great Manager has created a Great Team Culture. Such a manager should be appreciated and admired... rather than fired.

Perhaps the most revealing litmus test of a Great Team Culture is that you, the manager, feel comfortable in using the 2-5 weeks of vacation time that you've earned – *and enjoy it* – because you're not worrying about things falling apart in your absence. You are confident that your team is smart, reliable, caring, experienced, and efficient – and therefore can skillfully handle any emergencies that might come up while you're far, far away.

Safety net: You should leave instructions on how you can be contacted *in case of emergency* – but you can rest assured that your team will not bother you unless it's really urgent.

If you have created a Great Team Culture, they will take it as a challenge and as a matter of pride to *not* bother you when you're on vacation. That sends a very positive message to your Direct Reports: viz., that they are allowed to (and expected to) take worry-free vacations.

CHAPTER 67

WHAT IS THE ONE THING THAT NO ONE CAN TAKE FROM YOU?

G o on, take a guess.

Your favorite project? (Nope, the budget and staff for that project can be eliminated without advance notice.)

Your office location? (Nope, they can move you to another office, another building, another location, perhaps even another city or another country.)

The promotion and salary increase they promised you? (You're joking, right?)

Your position and title? (Such things can disappear in an instant.)

Your transitional object? (Just kidding...)

So I'll ask again: "What is the one thing that no one can take from you?"

Give up?

It's your **Integrity!** (If you have none left, you can skip to the next chapter.)

Notice that I didn't say "Honesty and Integrity", which are often lumped together. They are different entities. Here's the executive summary:

- *Honesty* does *not* subsume Integrity. Honesty connotes that you don't tell lies or intentionally mislead or deceive.
- *Integrity* subsumes Honesty. You can't have Integrity unless you're honest. However, Integrity is deeper and more complex than

Honesty: it's more than just about not lying. It's about the constellation of factors that define *character*.

What elements shape a person's character? Trustworthiness, responsiveness, consistency, altruism, transparency, empathy, fairness, predictability, putting the customer first, forthrightness, absence of deviousness, truthfulness (*aka* honesty)... and taking a solemn oath (spoken only to your inner self) to put your team's needs first. All these are part of what makes up your character, your Integrity.

You own your Integrity: it's the one thing in a work situation (or in your non-work life) that no one can take from you – because it lives inside of you, because no one in the company gave it to you. Nothing is more valuable (within a work context) than your Integrity. *Only you can give it away.*

Don't make the terrible mistake of forfeiting your integrity! Many people have... and lived to regret it mightily.

"Well, Jack, Aren't You Being a Little Simplistic, a Little Naïve?"

I understand that retaining your sense of integrity within a corporation can be difficult. You will often be caught between opposing forces. Bottom-line pressures and what seem to be temporary pressures can render ethics as a nice-to-have (rather than a must-have). Pressures can also lead to "circumvention" of ethical business practices.

You need to do your utmost to resist or alter circumstances that tempt you to temporarily abandon your best self and your sound judgments.

Warning: If you're forced to temporarily abandon your integrity more than once, start looking for your next position... because your current position is toxic.

"How Can I Tell If I'm Sacrificing My Integrity?"

If you don't think you can easily recognize that you are on the brink of handing over your integrity (or might already have done so) for the supposed "good of the company", here are some symptoms that will clue you in to your internal state of affairs:

- You have trouble falling asleep and staying asleep.
- You often wake up before your alarm goes off.
- You drink more alcohol than you used to... or are doing some other form of substance abuse.
- You eat more than you used to (perhaps snacking compulsively).
- You work longer hours than your previous long hours.
- You exercise less than you used to.
- You catch yourself being uncharacteristically curt with people, both at work and with friends and family outside of work.
- You're anxious a lot of the time, perhaps a little desperate, and you don't know why.
- You have physical symptoms (stress related?) that your physician can't diagnose.
- You have a vague sense (or perhaps a strong sense) of being depressed.
- Instead of enjoying your entire weekend, you start obsessing about work late Sunday afternoon and throughout Sunday evening.
- Your friends and/or your mate and/or your family keep asking, *"What's wrong?"* – because they have noticed a change in you, and they are concerned about you. And your repeated response is: *"Nothing. I'm fine. Just leave me alone."*

You might not have all these symptoms, but if you have more than a few, take notice!

Note: It might also be the case, even with your integrity intact, that you're not happy in your current work situation for a variety of reasons or that things are not going well outside of work – so this list of symptoms can be useful both at work and at home. It's important to try to assess the source of the symptoms.

Remember: *You own your Integrity.* No one can take it from you. Only you can give it away – and the cost of doing that is high... extraordinarily high.

PART THIRTEEN

CLOSING THOUGHTS

CHAPTER 68

Don't Forget the Golden Rule... Revised

I t's time to mention the Golden Rule... with a twist.

The Golden Rule, sometimes known as the "law of reciprocity", is often rendered in a form similar to: "Do unto others as you would have them do unto you."

But what if one of your Direct Reports or one of your peers likes to be treated in a manner different from the way you like to be treated?

One of my mentors – Lillian Malt *(see the "Remembrances" section later in this book)* – made an interesting and useful revision to the Golden Rule for use in the management workshops that we jointly facilitated. The revision takes into account that people are indeed different. Her version of the Golden Rule is:

"Do unto others as they would have you do unto them."

This amended version of the Golden Rule recognizes that not everyone thinks or feels in the way you think and feel – and that is something you need to always be conscious of if you aspire to be a Great Manager striving for a Great Team Culture.

Note: This amended Golden Rule does not apply to anyone who is a Bad Apple, or a cheat, or a liar, a con artist, or a narcissist.

CHAPTER 69

What's Love Got to Do with It?

D o you love your team? I hope you do… because that's a key indicator of a high-performance team and a Great Team Culture.

You might be wondering: *"What the heck is Jack talking about? Has he flipped out?"*

Well, love (a non-sexual sort, of course) has a *lot* to do with it. It's *your* team. You have created, or are creating, the team culture – so hopefully it's starting to look like the Great Team Culture that you envision. *(See Chapter 1: "Do I Have a Great Team Culture?")*

It's highly probably that you really like your team if the following are true:

- You look forward to and enjoy the team meetings you facilitate.
- You enjoy the 1-to-1 meetings with your Direct Reports.
- You wake up in the morning and look forward to coming to work.
- You take worry-free vacations because you know that you have a Great Team.

If you have inherited a team that has a culture different from the one you envision, then you'll have to figure out how to *transform the culture* into a Great Team Culture – so that you love coming to work and love working with your Direct Reports. Changing a team's culture is difficult – but doable. Here are some things that you'll need to consider if "culture change" is near the top of your to-do list:

- What are the characteristics of the team culture that I inherited?
- Do I want to maintain some of these characteristics? If 'yes', which ones?
- Are these characteristics traceable to the previous manager? Or are they traceable to one or two strong personalities that remain on the team? Or is the team culture a reflection of the overall company culture?
- What would my ideal team culture look and feel like? In what ways would it be different from the existing culture?
- Will my manager be supportive of the team culture I would like to create?

Warning: If your manager or skip-level manager formerly held your position and got promoted, then the existing team culture might be her/his doing – so you need to know who the previous manager was.

If your manager shaped the existing culture, you will need to tread *very carefully* in discussing the changes you'd like to bring about. It might be wisest to not discuss your desired changes... and instead fly under the radar and introduce changes in small steps rather than broadcast the long laundry list of cultural things that are wrong and that you plan to change.

- How, when, and where do I communicate to the team the type of team culture that I think is optimal for individual and team productivity and morale?
- How might I alter some of the structural elements of the team (e.g., team meetings, modes of communication)?
- What do I need to do on a 1-to-1 basis to bring about attitudinal change in one or more individuals on my team?
- How, when, and where do I model the behaviors that I would like my team to exhibit?

If you don't care deeply about your team, it's likely that you probably don't like the team culture that you inherited. If that's the case, you need to think long and hard about how to remedy the situation. This will be time well spent.

Moral of the story: If you don't love your team, you have work to do – so get to it.

CHAPTER 70

CONGRATULATIONS ! ! !

You've finished reading the whole book!!!

No? You didn't read the entire book word for word, line by line, page after page, chapter after chapter, all in one sitting? (I'm crushed.)

OK, OK, you are forgiven you if you skipped around, flipping pages and skimming paragraphs here and there, finding what was most relevant to your current situation (which is what I often do). That said...

... all is not lost. You can always go back and read the parts that you skipped at a time when those sections become more relevant to you.

GOOD LUCK in the next chapter of your work-life.

APPENDICES

INTRODUCTION

If you've been in your current managerial role for a while – say, more than 6 months – you can skip these "Mandatory Activities". That said, it might be useful to look them over quickly, as a refresher, just in case you might still be able to make good use of one or more of the activities.

If you are a new manager and if you skip any of the "mandatory" activities, you ought to have a strong reason for doing so. You can, of course, decide to move any mandatory activity to a different week – if that makes sense to you, given your situation.

WEEK 1 – MANDATORY ACTIVITIES

(If You've Recently Stepped into a Manager Role)

Activity	Why It's Important to Do	Done?

Send a "Hello" email to your team as soon as you arrive at your desk on Day 1.	Recall what you thought about and worried about when you heard that you were going to have a new manager... because your new Direct Reports will be having such thoughts. You need to calm them down by addressing their anxieties and curiosities as rapidly as possible. Ergo:
	
	• Your email should contain a friendly greeting (e.g., "Glad to be here... Looking forward to getting to know you and working with you...") and two specific points:
	  o Let them know that you'll be walking the hallways and just dropping in to say a brief "Hello" in person.
	  o Let them know that you'll be setting a date for an informal (non-business) team meeting.	

Walk the hallways during your first morning on the job to meet each Direct Report face-to-face.	• You want to just pop in each person's office, say "Hello" and "It's nice to meet you"... and get out of there. No agenda. Just human contact. Do *not* get drawn into a conversation about goals or assignments or what you're going to do differently. • Best Practice: Become a recurring "hallway walker", week after week after week.	

Schedule the first informal "hello team" meeting (to be held during Week 1).	• This first 30-minute team meeting should be held on your Day 2 or Day 3 on the job:
	  o 5 minutes for your self-intro
	  o 5 minutes to announce (no discussion) that:
	    ▪ You will schedule a meet-and-greet "ice breaker" team meeting;
	    ▪ You will schedule weekly recurring team business meetings;
	    ▪ You will schedule weekly recurring 1-to-1's.
	  o 20 minutes for Q&A (the team gets to grill you)	

Schedule the first, extra-long 1-to-1 meeting with each of your Direct Reports – and try to make that happen on Days 3-5 your during Week 1 on the job (and no later than during Week 2).	• This is a 90-minute 1-to-1 meeting… which you own. (Future 1-to-1 meetings are owned by your Direct Reports and will be 1 hour in length. You will schedule these as recurring weekly meetings – and your Directs will prepare/own the agenda.) • Schedule these initial 1-to-1's happen during the latter part of Week 1 or early Week 2 on the job… but *only after* the informal team meeting. (See previous item in this table.) • You own this meeting. • Use the template provided in the chapter titled *"What You Need to Learn at Your First (Atypical) 1-to-1 Meeting"*.	

Schedule the first formal business-oriented team meeting (for the following week).	• You are running a business, and your Direct Reports need to know how you will run that business and what their role in that business will be. • This meeting should take place during the middle of Week 2, after you've had a little bit of time to become familiar with your new territory.	
Schedule recurring weekly 60-minute 1-to-1's with each of your Direct Reports.	• The recurring 1-to-1's should occur *after* the first 90-minute 1-to-1 meeting (mentioned above). • Begin these recurring 1-to-1's in Week 2 or Week 3 of your tenure (but no later than in Week 3).	
Schedule the "Self-Intro" session (to be held in the 2nd or 3rd week of your tenure).	• This team meeting is a relaxed ice-breaker – to meet with your team on a human level (rather than a business level). • No formal business will be conducted at this meeting. • Instructions on how to facilitate this informal meeting are in *Chapter 8: Your First Team "Gathering"*.	

Week 2 – Mandatory Activities

(If You've Recently Stepped into a Manager Role)

Activity	Why It's Important to Do	Done?

Begin having the recurring 1-to-1 meetings with your Direct Reports.	• If you have not already scheduled the date/time for a recurring Weekly 1-to-1, try to set up at this meeting.
	• Begin, if possible, with the Direct Reports who have been on the team the longest.
	• If this is a new team, begin with the most senior members.
	• **TIP:** Do *not* read past Performance Review write-ups by your Directs' previous managers at this time. Read each Directs' resume before you meet for the first 1-to-1 that they own. After a month has gone by, *then* you can read their past Reviews.
	  ○ *"Why wait a month?"* Because you don't want to be prejudiced by a previous manager's point of view.
	  ○ The Direct and the previous manager might not have "clicked"... and the business situation might have been different... and the type of experience and skill-set required might have changed... and, and, and.
	  ○ Ergo, form your own opinion of your Direct Reports – and *then* read their past Performance Reviews.	

Begin scheduling lunches with your peers who report to the same manager (to occur within your first month on the job)... to occur in Week 3 and Week 4.	• Send out "Hello" emails to each of your peers (i.e., they report to the same manager that you report to), saying that you'd like to chat over lunch – and asking them to let you know when they have an opening on their calendar.
	• Schedule the lunch meetings for Week 3 and Week 4... because your peers are likely to be very busy people (as you are), so you need to plan a couple weeks ahead.
	    o Lunch meetings are preferred because chatting over lunch is a relaxed setting for developing good relationships.
	• You need to build good relationships with your peers ASAP:
	    o You will gain important insights about your manager, your skip-level manager, and the division.
	• You might have to collaborate with other managers who report to a different man-ager. Find out who these other managers are and try to have lunch with them.
	• **Caveat:** Do *not* schedule such meetings to occur in Week 1 or Week 2 because you will *not* yet know enough about your team, your business, and what's hap-pened in the past to make optimal use of your meetings.
	    By Week 3 you should know enough to ask your peers interesting questions that will round out your knowledge of the overall context within which you find yourself.	

Review existing Success Metrics.	• Review the past 2 years of performance against defined Success Metrics in order to develop a historical understanding of what strategies have and have not worked in this part of the corporation. Note which managers were in place 1-2 years ago.
	• If you study the Success Metrics, and if you think that the metrics are not actually *Success* Metrics (meaning: if you meet the metric, you definitely will have success), then share your point of view with your manager.
	    o Perhaps your manager will explain why the existing metrics are indeed Success Metrics.
	    o Perhaps your manager will agree with you... and ask you to craft metrics that more accurately and predictively identify success.
	    o In either case, this exercise will increase your understanding of the business that you are now managing – and also contribute to building a good working relationship with your manager.	

Review the presentations that your manager did in the past year or two.	• You need to understand how your manager is positioning the team within the larger organization. • Look for presentations by your manager to her/his unit. • Look for presentations by your manager to higher-ups. • Review the presentations in chronological order – from the oldest to the most recent.	

Review the presentations that your skip-level manager did in the past year or two.	• You need to understand the larger context that you're working within – as viewed by your skip-level manager. • Look for presentations by your skip-level manager to the unit and to higher-ups. • Review the presentations in chrono-logical order – from the oldest to the most recent.	

WEEK 3 – MANDATORY ACTIVITIES

(If You've Recently Stepped into a Manager Role)

Activity	Why It's Important to Do	Done?
Begin having lunch meetings with your peers who report to the *same* manager.	• It's critical that you have good working relationships with your peers because it will make life easier for your team – and greases the wheels for resolving unforeseen dilemmas. • In unity there is power: there will be times when you need to disagree with your manager's plans. If you are the only one not "with the program", you will lose the argument. However, if you and your peers have a united front and together express your concerns to your manager, you will win the argument a good percentage of the time... or your manager will have to fess up about the pressures coming from above. • These meetings should begin in Week 3... and should be concluded by Week 4.	
Begin scheduling lunches with your peers who report to a *different* manager.	• It's critical that you have good working relationships with peers in other units with whom your team collaborates. • Schedule the lunch meetings for Week 4 through Week 6.	

Review *again* the last pre-sentation that your manager gave (before you came on board)	• It's very important that you digest the substance of what your manager has communicated to the teams in her/his unit.	
Review *again* the last presentation that your skip-level manager gave (before you came on board)	• It's very important that you digest the substance of what your skip-level manager has communicated to the teams in the larger group.	
Review the last presentation that the CEO gave to the company.	• It's very important to understand the overall company context within which your team is operating.	

WEEK 4 – MANDATORY ACTIVITIES

(If You've Recently Stepped into a Manager Role)

Activity	Why It's Important to Do	Done?
Continue having lunch meetings with your peers who report to the *same* manager.	• These meetings should have begun in Week 3... and should be concluded by Week 4.	
Continue scheduling lunches with peers who report to a *different* manager.	• Such meetings will provide you with a bigger-picture context for where your team fit into the greater scheme of things. (You will also learn of job openings before they are posted.)	

Begin planning a 4-8 hour off-site meeting, to be held about 3 months into your stint as the new manager.	• You have wisely avoided making major changes (unless you were dropped into a mess that required you to make significant changes almost immediately). • Your team (and perhaps your manager) is wondering where you're going to lead the team. • Involve your team in this forward-thinking exercise... and start planning early because you want this meeting to be wildly successful – exciting, invigorating, collaborative, innovative, and productive. • The location should be different from your usual meeting place in a conference room. You need to get your team away from the daily distractions. • If you have a large team, consider hiring a facilitator.	
Initiate a deep-dive check-in with your manager when you have been in your manager role for 3 months.	• If you have not already done a detailed reality-check with your manager via 1-to-1 meetings, you need to have that. • You are seeking your manager's assessment of your performance to date. • Do *not* wait until a 6-month or 12-month performance review: you want to get your manager's blunt feedback so that you have plenty of time to course-correct if necessary.	

REMEMBRANCES... OF MENTORS PAST

I am grateful to many people who helped me along the way, some intentionally (via mentoring to one degree or another) or unintentionally (by modeling behavior that I observed and learned from). From these many people, three people deserve special recognition.

Eleanor (Elky) O. Shatzkin, a physicist by training, founded and ran the management consulting operation for the accounting firm J.K. Lasser, long before other large accounting firms created management-consulting practices. (And for a woman to be running such a practice in the late 1950s was highly unusual.) She went on to found her own management-consulting firm in mid-town Manhattan (very likely the first female sole-proprietor management consultant in New York City). Elky is the person who gave me a crash course in how businesses operate – from the front end (e.g., order taking, ticket-handling procedures, supply-chain management)... through intermediate processes (e.g., equipment and materials acquisition, inventory control, manufacturing procedures, scheduling, quality control, product finishing, problem-solving)... through the back end (e.g., packing, shipping, truck routing, receiving, handling returns). Under her tutelage, during summers while I was in college, I planned and executed the redesign and reorganization of seven departments of a shoe factory as well as developed a schedule-and-control system for a mid-sized Manhattan print shop, which had 4-color Harris presses that needed to be optimally utilized to turn a profit. To say that I learned a lot from Elky is an understatement.

Lillian G. Malt grew up in South Africa on a farm early in the 20th century. As a young adult she (a white woman in her early twenties) taught black children to read and do math in secret schools in the mid-20th century – and when that activity became dangerous, she fled the country... and went to London, where she specialized in skills analysis and training-program design while working at Pittman (as in, shorthand and other skills). She went on to found her own training and consulting firm in London, which specialized in ergonomics and training-program design. She taught me how to design training programs and how to design the far-more-challenging *re*-training programs by using a nuanced blend of skills-analysis methodology, ergonomic theory, learning theory, and neuro-muscular theory. She also drilled me in how to measure results and how to decide which results are worth measuring. I was given the opportunity to design products that work with (rather than against) human physiology. She provided me with one of the life lessons that helped transform me from a too-energetic, 20-something control freak into the first stage of working-adult maturity by repeatedly saying to me: *"Jack, stop running around trying to control everything. Control what you can control, and don't try to control what you can't control."* That was perhaps the most important of the many life lessons that I learned from Lillian... and it is advice that I sometimes need to remind myself to follow. (This is pretty good advice for intimate relationships, too.)

Jim Barrett was a master of marketing and sales, having cut his eye teeth at Xerox, which in the 1950s arguably had the best training programs in corporate America. He went on to become a vice president of marketing at Fairchild Semiconductor, where he trained and mentored many sales and marketing managers. He became president and CEO of Applied Learning Corporation, and he hired me as a senior trainer and senior consultant (when I was in my late 20s). I went on sales calls with him, ostensibly to provide technical input to detailed questions from potential clients – and in the process I learned a great deal about the art of client engagement. The most important thing that I learned from him was that you learn more from listening than from speaking. (Reminds me of a quote I memorized in high school: "When you speak, you are only repeating what you already know. If you listen, you might learn something.") By observing Jim, I learned from a pro how to listen closely to another person's comments, concerns, and questions – and to let what you learn from a client shape how you answer their questions and how you respond to their concerns. (No boilerplate "pitches".) That is an invaluable skill that I have used repeatedly throughout my life, both at work and in my private life.

I hope that the many "offspring" of Elky, Lillian, and Jim see these words and realize how fortunate they were to have known and been mentored by them. My gratitude to them runs deep.

●   ●   ●

I have also learned many things from many other people over the decades. They were not formal mentors, but they did things or said things or figured out things in ways that resonated with me – and that I absorbed into my way of being in the business world. In that way, I became a "scholar" of business strategy, management techniques, and business behavior. (Recall the old adage: "If you steal from one source, you're a plagiarist. If you steal from a few sources, you're a researcher. If you steal from many sources, you're a scholar.")

I do not want to forget the many wonderful people who were on my teams and the many wonderful people who were my peers and my managers, with whom I traded tips and techniques. Their critical and thoughtful feedback – their viewpoints, their encouragement, and sometimes their insistence that I and my team try harder and stretch further – were an integral part of my growth as a manager.

I thank all of them, living and dead, who shared their knowledge and taught me valuable life lessons.

Acknowledgments

Special thanks to Jeri L. Mersky, Ph.D. <jeri@jlmmc.com>, an experienced organizational consultant, who did a close read of the manuscript and provided much valuable feedback.

Thanks also to Darrel Stutesman and David Wertheimer, who read the entire manuscript and offered valuable suggestions, as well as to Kim Field, Thierry Paquay, and Tim Sinclair for urging me to broaden the focus of the book from *new* managers to *all* managers.

A heartfelt thanks to the dozens of people – too numerous to name – who offered encouragement to me all along the way.

I owe deep gratitude to my wife, Jane Ellis, a former law professor and psychoanalyst, a long-time fiction writer, and a most-expert editor, who flagged many issues (large and small) and made countless editorial suggestions. She also gently prodded me more than once when I was distracted from completing the manuscript – by reminding me of what I wanted this book to accomplish: viz., to make the world a better place to some slight degree by improving the workplace environment.

Finally, I take full credit for all flaws that remain in this book.

About the Author

Jack Litewka has over 40 years of management and consulting experience. He has worked in huge companies and small companies, in high tech and medium tech and low tech, and in for-profit and non-profit businesses.

During 14 years at Microsoft, he was a Sr. Director and Product Unit Manager – in the Windows Division (Microsoft.com, TechNet.com, MSDN.com, home.microsoft.com), in the MSN.com Division, in the Windows Media Division, and in the Worldwide Services Division. As part of the leadership brain trust in the Worldwide Services Division, he contributed to the strategy that grew a $500M business into a $1.5B business in less than 3 years. He and his team transformed a worldwide IT Professional training business from a $20M to a $60M business in less than 3 years. He was also the instigator of a company-wide mentoring program that has benefited thousands of Microsoft employees.

Over the decades Jack has mentored dozens of managers – and in that capacity he observed the many ways in which managers get into deep trouble or do a less-than-optimal job. This book draws on his one-to-one mentoring experience... to create a one-to-*many* mentoring experience.

In *The Sophisticated Manager: A Guide to Success,* Jack makes use of his substantial experience in turning around dysfunctional organizations as well as his coaching experience in helping new managers and experienced managers to progress to – and excel at – the next level in their careers.

"Jack is the best manager I have worked with in my 30-year career, and his advice should be taken to heart. His vast experience, positive approach, and resolute determination teach folks how to manage their teams effectively. He genuinely looks at a situation objectively, values his team's input, and decisively accomplishes the task at hand."

—Jeff Johnson, Partner Consultant

"I knew of Jack's reputation before even joining his organization, and then I was lucky enough to actually report to him. He has been my guide and mentor for many years. I learned things from Jack that I still count on today."

—Jane Dow, Sr. Technical Program Manager; formerly,
Sr. Group Site Manager for online businesses at
Microsoft

"Jack is one of those rare commodities in life: a man who can listen objectively and come up with intuitive ideas for one to consider when making life and career choices."

—Rayman Khan, IT Support Consultant

"Jack Litewka changed my life. About 35 years ago, we were colleagues when I became a single mother needing to make some big life changes. Jack brought his flip charts and colored markers to my house and led our team in a strategic planning session that focused, to my surprise, not only on my work situation but on my entire life. He asked the right questions and probed until I answered honestly.

"I was shocked to learn some of my hidden priorities that emerged that night. And the concrete steps needed that came out of that single session led to a turn in my career and a new job, literally within two weeks! Jack's work is unforgettable. Read his book."

—Marcia Antopol, Foundation Executive

"I am so grateful to Jack Litewka for providing us with his years of hands-on experience and organizational observations. The importance of effective managers at any level cannot be overstated. I have seen and been a part of organizations, from Fortune 500 to startup companies, where the necessary investments in manager training have not been made. This book is a great vehicle for empowering managers and positioning them for success.

"Jack offers tremendously valuable insights – important not only to new managers but also to veteran managers. When managers apply the tools and techniques Jack provides, they will be able to effectively utilize current talent while attracting additional world-class talent. I was fortunate to get a pre-publication peek at some of this book's chapters, and I have already benefited from his coaching."

—Eric King, Senior Manager, System Integration Architecture, Startup Company

"If you are a new manager, then I believe that you will find Jack Litewka's book to be extremely valuable. Based on my experience working with Jack, you will discover that this book is packed with insights based on his leadership skills and experience gained from building high-performance local teams or multi-million dollar global teams from the ground up or managing turn-arounds in a variety of industries."

—Eric Stathers, Managing Partner, Stathers & Associates LLC

"Jack is the best manager I have ever had in my 20 years of being employed. His team-building and individual-coaching methods bring out the best in a team. He instills absolute confidence in the team by working with them to provide a clear vision of what success looks like. But he also shares the good and the bad by being as transparent as possible, which creates a climate of trust."

—Rebecca Davis, Sr. Program Manager

"Jack Litewka is not your ordinary manager. During my 18+ years at Microsoft with 12 different managers, I learned that Jack sets himself apart by managing people, not projects. It's not that he forgets about the necessity of delivering well against commitments: it's just that project success flows naturally when an astute leader understands how to motivate and coach Direct Reports. My three years with Jack were terrific."

—*Steven Fox, Managing Director, Rollins Center for Entrepreneurship & Technology, Marriott School of Management, Brigham Young University; formerly, Director at Microsoft*

"When I needed to talk over issues with someone who was objective – issues such as cross-team coordination, dicey interpersonal situations, business strategy, and career choices – Jack was my go-to person. He offered sage advice as well as occasionally surprising, counter-intuitive advice – and was a valuable resource and mentor as I sorted through changing circumstances."

—*Ram Dixit, Sr. Director, at a Fortune 500 company*

"One of the key aspects for managers to succeed is having the right people on your team. But how do you crack the hiring code? How can you ask questions that interviewees can't prep for – so you get beyond the superficial? Jack has the answer. My first experience with Jack was when I was moving groups in Microsoft and Jack was on my interview loop. The previous interviews had been really easy, but when Jack started asking me questions I had to pause and think deeply before answering. Jack would then move to the next really probing question. I had never experienced anything like that before. He really made me sweat... and it was awesome. After I got the offer and moved to his group, I would constantly bounce ideas off Jack. I can't think of someone better qualified than Jack to give advice to new managers."

—*Ivan Joseph, Principal Program Manager at a Fortune 500 company*

"Jack is the best manager I have ever had in my 20 years of being employed. His team-building and individual-coaching methods bring out the best in a team. He instills absolute confidence in the team by working with them to provide a clear vision of what success looks like. But he also shares the good and the bad by being as transparent as possible, which creates a climate of trust."

—*Rebecca Davis, Sr. Program Manager*

"Jack's management style excelled in many ways. What stood out for me was how much trust and loyalty he built with the people that worked for him as well as from peers and management that depended on him. One "rule of respect towards others" that he had for himself was that if he was late to a meeting, he would not speak for as many minutes as he was late. He refused to be that person who would assume they knew the conversation and would just jump in with an opinion without knowing the context. Although he was rarely late, it was a noticeable show of respect that others rarely exercise and stood out so prominently that I recall that about him over 15 years later."

—*Todd Weeks, Vice President, Operations & Development*

"As a psychologist, I'm always seeking useful readings for my clients. Trying to balance work, life and the evolving dynamics of the modern business world can take its toll. *The Sophisticated Manager* hits the mark. Mr. Litewka applies his keen intelligence and years of managerial experience and insights to offer managers a wealth of strategies and practical advice. He is a great teacher and writer.

"I particularly appreciated his "in the trenches" approach, and discovered many useful ideas and tools to help my clients. I highly recommend this book."

—*Steven Walch, Ph.D., Clinical Psychologist*

"As the creator of several successful ventures, Jack Litewka is a brilliant example of how you build businesses with people. In Jack you find a creative intellect with a strong emphasis on practical action. Jack reveals highly insightful business thinking, always balanced with sensitivity for people.

"Jack is an inspiring person to work for – and it's great to now have his thoughts on the process of management written down, for the benefit of a wider audience."

—Andrew Delin, Principal Consultant, ICT management / Product & Service Planning and Delivery

"When Jack took on the management of our large, multi-disciplinary Web team, he brought welcome measures of wholeness and humanity to a highly technical, high-pressure workplace. He deftly managed up, artfully managed down, and elicited some of the best work of our careers. It was a great experience, with lots of lessons of real and lasting value.

"And for those of us with teams of our own, Jack's leadership and insights made better managers of us all."

—Larry Sisson, Director, User Experience Planning & Architecture; formerly, Group Manager at Microsoft

"Jack and I worked together in a "sink or swim" culture where leadership and coaching were very rare. Jack has a gift for developing his people through providing guidance as necessary and offering ample personal growth opportunities."

— Alan Wong, Director of Product Marketing, Asia; formerly, Sr. Director at Microsoft

"Jack is that rare breed of manager who is valued equally – and highly – by his employees, his peers, and his leadership teams. Jack sees and nurtures potential in people. He challenges his team and helps them succeed. Careers blossom under Jack.

"As a peer, Jack is the voice of reason you want in a critical meeting. He is unafraid to ask the hard questions or take an unpopular stance if he believes it's right. The logic he brings to the conversation is calm and compelling. His input inevitably leads to better decisions."

—Barbara Roll, Content Marketing / Digital Strategy; formerly, Online Marketing Director and Group Program Manager at Microsoft

"Jack is one of the only managers I have worked for who was able to integrate poetry into team meetings in a way that provided a certain level of mystery. He managed people at a high level of purpose and intention, and I am very fortunate to have had the opportunity to learn from him early in my career."

—Taylor Parsons, Sr. Product Manager

"Jack Litewka was truly my favorite manager at Microsoft. He was responsible for home.microsoft.com and msn.com home pages – and the team morale was among the highest I've experienced anywhere. I look forward to reading Jack's book to find out how he did it. At the time I felt it had something to do with his humanity, integrity, and background as a poet."

—Pam Kilborn-Miller; formerly, Program Manager for MSN.com Home

"The book is extremely useful, easy to absorb, and a really good read. I had the opportunity to review some chapters before publication – and I couldn't put it down. It is world-class work!"

— *Tim Sinclair, General Manager at a Fortune 500 company, Big Data and Business Intelligence, China Market*

"I had the honor to work with Jack in the Worldwide Services business. Jack built and led a large senior team and fostered an incredibly positive environment for his employees to thrive in while innovating the business for profitability. I was truly inspired by Jack's leadership and his approach as a people manager – and the most senior lead on our leadership team. Often times, Jack mentored and coached his peers at times of team conflict, demonstrating concern for and awareness of the broader team dynamics (beyond the people he directly managed).

"Jack was the voice of wisdom as a people leader. He helped us all grow in our careers. His strategic approach in building a worldwide services business from the ground up resulted in very high customer satisfaction around the globe – and a very healthy profit margin."

— *Yonca Yalcin Spinelli, Director, HP Alliance Global Channel Business*

CPSIA information can be obtained
at www.ICGtesting.com
Printed in the USA
LVOW13s0001151216
517344LV00029B/344/P